T0339726

Cambridge Elements ≡

Elements in the Philosophy of Immanuel Kant
edited by
Desmond Hogan
Princeton University
Howard Williams
University of Cardiff
Allen Wood
Indiana University

RATIONALIZING
(VERNÜNFTELN)

Martin Sticker
*University of Bristol and Kantian Rationality Lab &
Academia Kantiana, Immanuel Kant Baltic Federal
University*

CAMBRIDGE
UNIVERSITY PRESS

CAMBRIDGE
UNIVERSITY PRESS

University Printing House, Cambridge CB2 8BS, United Kingdom

One Liberty Plaza, 20th Floor, New York, NY 10006, USA

477 Williamstown Road, Port Melbourne, VIC 3207, Australia

314–321, 3rd Floor, Plot 3, Splendor Forum, Jasola District Centre, New Delhi – 110025, India

103 Penang Road, #05–06/07, Visioncrest Commercial, Singapore 238467

Cambridge University Press is part of the University of Cambridge.

It furthers the University's mission by disseminating knowledge in the pursuit of education, learning, and research at the highest international levels of excellence.

www.cambridge.org
Information on this title: www.cambridge.org/9781108714426
DOI: 10.1017/9781108625661

First published 2021

A catalogue record for this publication is available from the British Library.

ISBN 978-1-108-71442-6 Paperback
ISSN 2397-9461 (online)
ISSN 2514-3824 (print)

Rationalizing (*Vernünfteln*)

Elements in the Philosophy of Immanuel Kant

DOI: 10.1017/9781108625661
First published online: December 2021

Martin Sticker
*University of Bristol and Kantian Rationality Lab & Academia Kantiana,
Immanuel Kant Baltic Federal University*

Author for correspondence: Martin Sticker, martin.sticker@bristol.ac.uk

Abstract: Kant was a keen psychological observer and theorist of the forms, mechanisms and sources of self-deception. In this Element, the author discusses the role of rationalizing/*Vernünfteln* for Kant's moral psychology, normative ethics and philosophical methodology. By drawing on the full breadth of examples of rationalizing Kant discusses, the author shows how rationalizing can extend to general features of morality and corrupt rational agents thoroughly (albeit not completely and not irreversibly). Furthermore, the author explains the often-overlooked roles common human reason, empirical practical reason and even pure practical reason play for rationalizing. Kant is aware that rationality is a double-edged sword; reason is the source of morality and of our dignity, but it also enables us to seemingly justify moral transgressions to ourselves, and it creates an interest in this justification in the first place. Finally, this Element discusses whether Kant's ethical theory itself can be criticised as a product of rationalizing.

Keywords: Kant, ethics, self-deception, reason, authority of morality

ISBNs: 9781108714426 (PB), 9781108625661 (OC)
ISSNs: 2397-9461 (online), 2514-3824 (print)

Contents

1 Introduction 1

2 Rationalizing in Context 4

3 Rationalizing and the Natural Dialectic 14

4 The Cunning of (Empirical Practical) Reason 23

5 Apparent Justifications, Ideology and Uncritical Philosophy 37

6 Whose Rationalizing? 50

Abbreviations 60

References 62

1 Introduction

For without philosophy, nowadays only criminals dare to hurt other humans.
(Robert Musil, *Der Mann ohne Eigenschaften*, ch. 48; author's translation)

L'hypocrisie est un hommage que le vice rend à la vertu.
(François de la Rochefoucauld, *Réflexions ou sentences et maximes morales et réflexions diverses*, Maxim 218)

So convenient it is to be a reasonable creature, since it enables one to find or make a reason for everything one has a mind to do.
(Benjamin Franklin, *The Life of Benjamin Franklin: An Autobiographical Manuscript*, p. 43)

The key thing with resolutions is not to keep them. It's how to revise them once you fail.
(John Oliver on New Year's resolutions)

This Element combines two of my long-standing philosophical interests: the ethics of Immanuel Kant and misuses of rational capacities. The significance of the latter phenomenon stretches far beyond Kant scholarship. For instance, one of the most memorable moments of my student days was when one of my professors claimed that 'Ethicists are the worst people in the world because they know all the excuses'. I think this is a somewhat pessimistic – though, as we will see, very Kantian – thought.

According to Immanuel Kant's biographer Manfred Kuehn (2001: 222), Kant 'had formulated the maxim for himself that he would smoke only one pipe [a day], but it is reported that the bowls of his pipes increased considerably in size as the years went on'. Kant's implementation of his own maxim is here in tension with the aim incorporated into this maxim, which presumably was to limit tobacco consumption. Kant treats the maxim as an externally imposed constraint that must be obeyed to the letter, but not in spirit. The implementation undermines his end without formally renouncing it. Kuehn's anecdote, though it concerns matters of prudence rather than morality, nicely illustrates the subject matter of this Element: quibbling with rules, trying to outsmart one's better self or, as Kant calls it, *vernünfteln*/'rationalizing', understood as the use of rational capacities to undermine reason, or an exercise of reason that weakens agents' readiness to do the right thing while they yet deem themselves committed to morality.

Kant was a keen psychological observer of this phenomenon, and the dangers it poses are a major theme in his moral philosophy. Consequently, his discussion of rationalizing will help us to better understand a number of important aspects of his philosophy. First, practical philosophy is supposed to function as an 'antidote' (Wood 2002: 28) against rationalizing. Understanding rationalizing will illuminate the *purposes that moral principles and theories serve*, and will help us to understand what the role of the philosopher is for moral improvement.[1] Second, the concept of rationalizing is central for our understanding of Kant's engagement with his *academic colleagues and the popular philosophers* whom he considers to advocate sophisticated forms of rationalizing. Moreover, he criticizes religious institutions and practices because they propagate and encourage mistaken beliefs about moral responsibility.[2] Third, Kant's discussions of concrete examples of rationalizing offer instructive *case studies for how our moral reasoning can go wrong*. A detailed look at these examples will enhance our understanding of Kant's conception of the workings as well as deficits of our rational faculties. Fourth, throughout his discussions of the various *dialectics* that our reason is subject to and that necessitate critiques of our rational capacities, Kant describes fundamental mistakes in reasoning labelled 'rationalizing'.[3] Kant is interested in the impact of rationalizing on all aspects of our use of reason. However, due to constraints of space, I will focus on the practical dimension.

In this Element, I will take a detailed look at the examples Kant provides of rationalizing, at his own explanations of the underlying process and at the

---

[1] Wood (2017: 20–6, 74) correctly stresses that Kant's ethics is not primarily supposed to serve a theoretical or intellectual purpose, but to address *moral* flaws. Most recently Callanan (2019) has argued that the discussion of the natural dialectic, in which Kant introduces rationalizing, is central to a correct understanding of the *Groundwork*. Kant here parts way with Rousseau who is sceptical that philosophy can ever help agents to become and remain moral, whereas Kant argues that philosophy can and must perform this function.

[2] We can find a secular example for this phenomenon in a *New Yorker* cartoon in which a number of men in a business meeting ask their secretary, Miss Dugan, to send in an expert who can tell right from wrong. Wood (2017: 17), from whom I take this example, analyzes this as follows. These men 'are about to do something they know is wrong. Yet they are tempted to do it anyway, no doubt on the ground that doing it serves "the greater good" (the firm's, the university's, or just their own). They are in a quandary because they are tempted to think that this "greater good" might justify (perhaps only "just this once") their doing what [. . .] they know perfectly well is wrong. The call to Miss Dugan is an admission that, in their condition of moral weakness, the shallow "cognitive" (i.e., the "cost–benefit" or "greater good") part of their brains has so disoriented their good judgment that they no longer know what they know and what they don't. But at least they do know that they no longer know what they know; that last pitiful shred of human decency shows itself in their desperate plea for help, comically masquerading as a dignified professional request for outside expertise.' There are many other contemporary examples from politics, public discourse, and the private sector as well as institutions of education to which Kant's analysis of rationalizing applies.

[3] This is most apparent for the natural dialectic in G, IV: 404.37–405.19, which I will discuss in detail in Section 3. In the First Critique, rationalizing is presented as an exercise of rational capacities without awareness of their dialectical nature, resulting in antinomical claims (A/B: 422/450; see also A/B: 63/87–8, 421/448–9). In the Third Critique, Kant explains rationalizing as the act of claiming a priori universality for one's judgements, which can lead to a dialectic of opposing judgements (CJ, V: 337.5–8; see Section 2.1).

effects rationalizing has on agents' grasp of morality, and will discuss the necessary conditions for rationalizing to be possible and to appear as a promising strategy to agents for dealing with moral commands that can require great sacrifice from them. In doing so, I aim to shéd new light on Kant's philosophy in a number of ways.

(1) The main contribution of this Element is to challenge the widely shared assumption that rationalizing in Kant only extends to *questions of motivation and specific maxims*. By drawing on the full breadth of examples of rationalizing presented by Kant, I will show how rationalizing can lead to a systematically distorted sense of right and wrong which Kant labels 'corruption'. When I rationalize, I undermine the grasp that the supreme principle of morality has on me, while I still believe myself fully committed to morality, albeit to a less demanding moral principle or more lenient conception of morality. There is much more to rationalizing than misrepresenting the strength or source of motives.

(2) I explain in what sense rationalizing is a *rational* activity. Empirical practical reason devises pseudo-justifications and finds excuses to promote an agent's sensuous ends at the expense of morality. Paradoxically, the interest in these pseudo-justifications is rooted in rational agents' recognition of the authority of morality. Only agents who recognize the authority of morality are tempted to look for excuses or apparent justifications for their morally dubious actions. My discussion will reveal that Kant is not an arch-rationalist who believes in the power of reason without qualification.[4] Kant understands that moral failings are not simply the fault of inclinations and of our sensuous side (in fact, they are never simply that). Many instances of moral failure are expressions of fallacious (but not always obviously incorrect) reasoning and even of forms of pseudo-rationality that can be extremely sophisticated. Kant is aware that rationality is a double-edged sword; it is the source of morality and of our dignity, but it also enables us to seemingly justify moral transgressions to ourselves and others, and it creates an interest in such justifications in the first place.

(3) I explain how it is possible for a rationalizer to think that committing a moral violation can be *excused* and even *justified*, even though this rationalizer has not completely lost touch with the moral law. This will allow us to

---

[4] That Kant was blindly optimistic about the power of reason is a stereotype that still prevails at least among non-specialists. See, for instance, Haidt (2001), who discusses Kant under the label 'Worship of Reason', and Mercier and Sperber (2018: 17), who count Kant as a philosopher who assumes that 'humans err by not reasoning enough', not by 'reasoning too much'.

maintain that rationalizers are still moral agents and are morally responsible for their actions. It will also demonstrate that Kant does not think that corrupted agents are merely in a state of confusion in which they feel a need for urgent philosophical help. They can be in a state of false (though never complete) certainty.

(4) I will close with a *critical discussion* of the scope and underlying assumptions of Kant's conception of rationalizing. Such a critical discussion is pivotal, since Kant criticizes competing ethical theories for being rationalizations and for reinforcing and encouraging rationalizing. Understanding whether charging a philosopher with rationalizing is a valid criticism, and understanding whether Kant is in a position to level this criticism against other theorists, will help us gain a better general understanding of the strengths and weaknesses of Kant's ethics.

2 Rationalizing in Context

I begin with a few remarks about the term 'rationalizing' (Section 2.1) and about common themes in the literature on rationalizing and self-deception (Section 2.2); I then outline why rationalizing is an important concern specifically in the context of Kant's *practical* philosophy (Section 2.3).

2.1 *Vernünfteln*

The nouns *Vernünfteln, Vernünftelei* and *Vernünftelung*, as well as the verb *vernünfteln*, were in much more frequent use in the eighteenth century than they are in contemporary German, where the term is largely out of use. *Vernünfteln* is composed of *Vernunft* (reason), and the suffix *eln*. This suffix indicates that *Vernünfteln* is an activity. It is also a diminutive (see Adelung 1811: vol. 3, col. 1785), which gives *Vernünfteln* negative connotations in the sense of using reason in a deficient manner. According to Grimm and Grimm (1889: vol. 25, col. 936–9), *Vernünfteley* (noun) is an 'incorrect and inappropriate use of reason', and *vernünfteln* (verb) means 'presenting something as seemingly correct, which is in itself pedantic and incorrect' (my translations).

Kant himself explains the meaning of the term twice. According to the Third Critique, *Vernünfteln* is the act of claiming a priori universality for one's judgements, which can lead to a dialectic of opposing judgements (CJ, V: 337.5–8): 'A rationalizing judgment (*iudicium ratiocinans*) is any judgment that declares itself to be universal' (CJ, V: 337fn.). *Vernünfteln* here is a necessary but not sufficient condition for dialectical reasoning. Only judgements claiming a priori universality can give rise to a dialectic. However, many judgements claiming a priori universality do not lead to a dialectic.[5] After all, their claims might be justified. *Vernünfteln* here seems to not be inherently problematic. By contrast, in the *Anthropology*, 'Vernünfteln (without sound reason)' is defined as 'use of reason that misses its final goal, partly from inability, partly from an inappropriate viewpoint' (Anth, VII: 200.5–7). *Vernünfteln*, if not constrained by sound reason, is here presented as a use of reason that, by definition, produces incorrect results. Moreover, *Vernünfteln* is presented as of a much broader scope, since it is not necessarily tied to claims to (a priori) universality and it can result in all kinds of mistakes, not all of which have to be dialectical.

Kant's actual use of the term is even broader than what the *Anthropology*'s definition indicates. He sometimes uses the term to simply mean 'reasoning' or 'reflection' without any negative connotations. This is presumably the case when *Vernünfteln* is constrained by, or in the service of, sound reason.[6] In many cases, *Vernünfteln* does, however, indicate a *deficient* use of rational capacities,[7] and I will discuss in Section 3.1 whether this deficiency involves a dialectics in the terminological sense. Furthermore, Kant sometimes uses other terms to mean the same as *Vernünfteln*, occasionally using *vernünfteln* and *räsonniren* interchangeably (Anth, VII: 200.10),[8] and he stresses that humans 'artificialize' [*künsteln*] in order to represent moral transgressions as an 'unintentional fault'

---

[5] Cf. also Guyer and Matthews (2000: 213): a rationalizing judgement connotes 'only a necessary condition of a sophistical argument, namely that it make a pretense to universality, without yet implying that anything that gives rise to a dialectic is sophistical in the usual, pejorative sense'. Kant distinguishes between a rationalizing judgement and a rational judgement [*Vernunfturteil*] (CJ, V: 337fn.). Only the latter is grounded a priori as it is the conclusion of a rational inference, whereas a rationalized judgement is the major premise of such an inference. Kant also frequently distinguishes 'rationalizing' from 'rational' (A/B, 340/398, 604/632; CJ, V: 396.7–16; RO, XX: 179.12–15).

[6] There is no German word equivalent to the English 'reasoning' or 'reasoner' in the sense that it is a cognate of 'reason'/*Vernunft* and indicates the use someone makes of reason or the person who reasons. Obviously, there are terms for this (e.g., *denken* and *Denker*) but these terms are not etymologically connected to reason. The closest German comes to such terms is *vernünfteln/* 'rationalizing' and *Vernünftler/*'rationalizer'. Kant sometimes uses these terms to simply refer to 'reasoning' and 'reasoners'. I am grateful to Thomas Sturm for discussion of these etymological points.

[7] For examples of deficient uses of reason characterized as 'rationalizing', see A/B: 269/325–6; MFNS, IV: 505.25–31, 523.25–9; CJ, V: 262.24–5; MM, VI: 215.36–216.6; Anth, VII: 119.14–22, 201.12–23, 228.16–18; Men, VIII: 151.19–25; MPT, VIII: 267.18–22; TP, VIII: 301.1–15; TPP, VIII: 382.15–21; PCT, VIII: 416.3–9; Corr, X: 432.4–11; FI, XX: 234.12–24; PM, XX: 343.10–14; RE, XX: 412.13–413.11; P-PR, XX: 437.1–438.3; L-Men, XXV: 1041.28–1042.3; Eth-K: 127–9.

[8] However, often *räsonniren* is used to describe harmless arguments during dinner (Anth, VII: 280.10–19) or reasoning without sufficient insight into underlying principles (Anth, VII: 200.10–12, 476.31–4). Likewise, 'empty musing' [*leere Grübelei*] (Anth, VII: 221.30) and 'cheeky musings' [*vorwitzige Grübeleien*] (CF, VII: 24.2) indicate comparatively harmless shortcomings.

or mere 'oversight' (CPrR, V: 98.13–21)[9] and that they can 'bully' [*chicanie-ren*] their conscience (G, IV: 404.21; see also Eth-V, XXVII: 620.3).[10] Moreover, Kant refers to a vain or pointless exercise of rational capacities as *herausklügeln* (Rel, VI: 26fn.), which literally means 'to prudentialize something out of something'. Kant, while not usually known for his literary style, clearly shows great enthusiasm for the creative use of language when describing misuses of reason.

Vernünfteln has been translated in various ways.[11] I will follow Timmermann (2011) and use 'rationalizing', as it makes clear that *Vernünfteln* is an exercise of rational capacities. 'Rationalizing', as I will use the term, is self-deception about *moral* matters. There are other kinds of self-deception, such as about what is prudent, one's capabilities and social standing and maybe even about purely theoretical questions. Self-deception about these issues, however, requires a framework different from the one that explains rationalizing in my sense, since these other forms of self-deception are not driven by a rational interest in being morally justified (see Section 4.3).

I should note that 'rationalizing', as I will use the term, is broader than the rational-tail-wagging-the-emotional-dog manoeuvre of finding post hoc justifications for decisions driven by emotions.[12] That rationalizing is post hoc and preceded by judgement is a frequent assumption especially in psychological approaches to the phenomenon (see, for instance, Cushman 2020: 1).[13] Rationalizing in Kant is not merely a matter of finding post hoc justifications. Misconceptions about morality can inform ex ante reasoning and can influence judgements and overturn agents' decisions – but not change them for the better (see Sections 4.5 and 5.2). Moral judgements, for Kant, are never merely driven by emotions, since a judgement is always a cognitive act. Yet, moral judgements can be incorrect and rationalized. Moreover, agents rationalize not merely to feel better about their judgements or to make their own actions comprehensible

---

[9] According to the *Kaehler Notes*, 'artificializing' [*künsteln*] is supposed to modify one's representation of morality 'until it conforms to the inclinations and leisureliness' (Eth-K: 356).

[10] I owe the references to *chicanieren* to Di Giuolio (2020: 277–8). Timmermann's (2011: 36) translation, 'engage in legalistic quibbles', makes the connection to rationalizing more apparent but is somewhat free.

[11] For instance: 'quibbling' (Timmermann 2007: 48), 'subtle reasoning' (Gregor 1996: 139), 'sophistical' (Gregor 1996: 649; see also Guyer and Wood 1998: 629), 'sophistry' (Wood and Di Giovanni 1998: 88), 'subtle argument' (Wood and Di Giovanni 1998: 99), 'ratiocination' (Wood and Di Giovanni 1998: 144), 'rationalistic' (Guyer and Matthews 2000: 213), 'reasoning' (Guyer and Matthews 2000: 371), 'pseudorationality' (Kemp Smith 1933: 327).

[12] See Haidt's (2001) influential article in which he argues that most of our moral judgements are driven by emotions, and that justifications are only obtained post hoc.

[13] However, Ellis and Schwitzgebel (2020: 23) note that *'rationalization in the pejorative sense'*, that is, when it leads to morally criticizable behaviour, is typically prior to a moral judgement and seeks to vindicate the option already favoured by the agent (see also Sievers 2020).

to themselves, but because they genuinely do acknowledge the authority of reason (Section 4.3).

2.2 Rationalizing in Kant: The State of the Art

Kant's frequent use of the term *Vernünfteln*[14] is in stark contrast to the neglect this term has received in the literature until recently. Caygill's (1995) and Holzhey and Mudroch's (2005) Kant dictionaries lack any entry on *Vernünfteln*, Eisler (1930) only quotes a single passage (namely, CJ, V: 337) and König's article on *Vernünfteln* in the recent *Kant-Lexikon* (Willaschek et al. 2015) does not even mention Kant's practical philosophy.[15]

More recently, however, there has been increased interest in rationalizing, and a number of publications have presented sophisticated textual and systematic reconstructions of rationalizing in Kant and highlighted the significance of this concept for Kant's philosophy. Among these publications, three approaches are especially noteworthy for my own.

First, Laura Papish (2018: ch. 3) stresses that rationalizing centrally involves phenomena such as quibbling with things for which we have overwhelming evidence (74–9). For her, rationalizing is a violation of *epistemic norms* and it primarily impacts questions of justification.[16] I agree with Papish's focus on matters of justification and, in fact, one of my main quarrels especially with older literature on the topic (see below in this section) is the widespread

---

[14] The search engine of the online *Kant-Korpus*, which contains the first twenty-three volumes of the *Academy Edition*, gives thirty-five hits for *Vernünfteln* (noun), twenty for *Vernünfteley/ Vernünftelei* (noun), eighteen for *Vernünftler* (noun), seventy for *vernünfteln* (verb) and forty for *vernünftelnd* (adjective). This does not include exotic compounds such as *herausvernünfteln* (CPrR, V: 31.26; OAD, VIII: 220.33; MPT, VIII: 264.12), *wegvernünfteln* (G, IV: 456.2; CPrR, V: 154.3; PM, XX: 279.5) and *übervernünfteln* (MPT, VIII: 265f.26). In comparison, *factum* [*Faktum*] in the sense of 'fact of reason', a central term for Kant's ethics from the Second Critique onwards, only occurs eighteen times in its terminological sense (CPrR, V: 6, 31, 32, 42, 43, 47, 55, 91, 104; MM, VI: 252; Corr, XI: 58, 340; Corr, XII: 21; Ref, XIX: 612; OP, XXI: 21, 25, 36). Of the fifty-five quotes that Grimm and Grimm's (1889: vol. 25, col. 936–9) entry on *Vernünfteln* provides, thirty-three are from Kant's works alone. Kant was evidently particularly fond of this term even when the term was still in wider use than today.

[15] Most recently, Callanan (2019: 4) stressed that there 'has been surprisingly little analysis of the mechanism of the natural dialectic', rationalizing among them.

[16] Allais (2021: 49) also stresses epistemic failings, such as 'screening off' certain considerations. Of course, violations of epistemic norms can have important practical implications. Papish (2018: 110) argues that 'devotion to self-love becomes entrenched insofar as self-deception enables self-love to stake out new territory that it did not previously have and that outstrips our initial commitment to securing more banal and immediate objects of desire'. See also Wehofsits (2020), who argues that rationalizing can increase the hold of passions on an agent by revaluating and elevating their normative status, which 'leads to more comprehensive cognitive distortions' (14). The real danger of rationalizing is not that it seemingly licenses one-off transgressions, but its broader impact on agents' reasoning and character (see also Section 5).

assumption that rationalizing is merely or mainly a matter of misinterpreting one's motivation rather than of judging incorrectly about what one ought to do.

Moreover, Papish claims that it is one of the 'most important features of Kant's approach to self-deception [. . .] that reason is constitutively incapable of' rationalizing such that a rationalizer forms 'a particular belief according to which laxness and impurity are permitted' (2018: 84). Rather, laxness and impurity enter indirectly 'by means of the diversion of attention toward some pleasing alternative cognition' (2018: 84). In contrast to Papish, I do think that it is possible that rationalizers explicitly endorse a lax and impure conception of morality. In fact, I believe that this is what Kant suspects has happened to many of his academic colleagues who postulate happiness as the source of morality. I will present a theory of rationalizing that seeks to fully account for the potentially devastating impact that this activity can have on our understanding of morality and that can explain how agents can come to confidently assert overly lenient conceptions of morality and to even defend them against reasonable criticism.

I suspect that the differences between Papish's and my take on rationalizing are due to our respective focus on different paradigms of rationalizing. Papish approaches the phenomenon from relatively everyday cases that we find in the political and social sphere.[17] By contrast, I focus chiefly on more extreme cases that we can find in Kant's discussion of eudaemonists and of religious practices. In these cases, it becomes apparent that Kant does allow for the possibility of very corrupted agents who are more than merely confused about morality. My reading, I believe, can make better sense of the way Kant seeks to address rationalizing, namely via his ethical theory. If rationalizing was primarily a violation of epistemic requirements, then we would expect Kant to present guides to good *thinking* in order to combat this failing. However, Kant thinks that specifically 'practical grounds' compel us 'to take a step into the field of a *practical philosophy*' (G, IV: 405.22–4). We need *ethical* theory to address rationalizing, because rationalizing, in its most dangerous form, involves false beliefs specifically about morality and lack of commitment to the correct moral principles. Having said this, however, I should note that I regard Papish's and my approach largely as complementary in the sense that we focus on different paradigmatic cases of the same phenomenon. Moreover, Papish's discussion of

---

[17] Papish's (2018: 74–5) chief examples from Kant are the *political moralist* who brings up supposed empirical evidence against the (non-empirical) proposition that people should unite into a just state (TPP, VIII: 378), shifting to *irrelevant questions* in order to distract from the real issues (MM, VI: 318) and *switching between roles* as a private and official person (WIE, VIII: 37).

the epistemic dimensions of rationalizing constitutes a major contribution to our understanding of the phenomenon.

Second, Jeanine Grenberg (2013) presents an innovative new reading of the methods and aims of Kant's ethics, which she claims is centred on the first-person perspective of an agent experiencing respect for the moral law. As part of her investigation into the perspective of the agent, Grenberg extensively discusses rationalizing and corruption as the main threats to an agent's grasp of morality. One of her central claims is that even the corrupt person must still retain '*some* sense of the superior authority of moral principles, at least enough to realize she needs help maintaining that authority' (2013: 93). I agree with her that rationalizing would not make sense for an agent who does not recognize the authority of morality, and in Section 4 (especially 4.3) I will explain why this is so. However, I will also argue that while corrupted agents can be brought to doubt their mistaken views, Kant is not committed to the claim that all rationalizers acknowledge or feel the need for philosophical help. Rationalizing is dangerous because it can result in *false certainty*. Understanding this false certainty will help us understand why external help is important for agents, and the kind of help required.

Third, in a paper on the objection of 'moral overdemandingness', Marcel van Ackeren and Martin Sticker (2014: sec. 3) propose that Kant would consider it 'a model case of a rationalizing attack on our ordinary understanding of morality' that 'some contemporary philosophers consider high demandingness of a theory as something that calls for revision of this theory' (86).[18] They suggest that Kant could respond to an overdemandingness objection by showing how those who level the objection are, in fact, engaged in rationalizing. In Section 6, I will critically discuss whether rationalizing can indeed function as a response to objections of overdemandingness and as a criticism of lenient moral theories.

In addition to the current interest specifically in the concept of rationalizing, there is also ongoing discussion of this phenomenon under the more general label of *self-deception*. Literature on this topic has done much to stress the significance of this phenomenon particularly for Kant's framework,[19] especially with regard to self-deception about motives. In fact, it is a widespread assumption that self-deception in Kant is a matter of misrepresenting the motivation of one's actions. For instance, Nelson Potter (2002: 386) points out the 'centrality

---

[18] A similar charge, without appeal to Kant, was levelled by Wilson (1993: 278), who criticizes the overdemandingness objection as 'an ideology of academicians who are now, in a way they have never been before, part of a materially favored class'.

[19] See, for instance, Piper (1988: 298), who states that for Kant 'the really pressing motivational problem for actual moral agents is not *akrasia*, but rather self-deception', and Grenberg (2010: 162), who argues that an ethical approach, which deems vicious acts to be free and rational, 'requires a moment of rationalization, or even self-deception, in order to work'.

and overwhelming significance of self-deception' as 'a subterranean theme in Kant's moral philosophy', where self-deception takes the form of either deceiving oneself about the *strength* of moral motives (387) or as 'the self-deception by which we tell ourselves that we are acting for high and purely moral motives, when our real motives relate to self-love' (388).[20]

Associating self-deception with misrepresenting one's motives, of course, makes a lot of sense in the context of a philosophy that both stresses the importance of the right motivation for moral worth and maintains the ultimate opacity of our motives (see Section 4.3). However, I think it is very significant that rationalizing does not merely pertain to presenting oneself as having acted for high and mighty reasons. Since Kant's theory of rationalizing is scattered throughout his works, it is easy to miss the full extent to which he analyzes different forms of rationalizing, as well as its moral, psychological and social dimensions. That rationalizing, besides motivation, affects an agent's reasoning and general understanding of morality is pivotal for Kant, as rationalizing is supposed to function as an explanation for how it is possible that rational agents, capable of moral cognition, can have false beliefs about morality, think that their moral violations are justified and even advocate mistaken moral theories.

Finally, I should mention that it is telling that Kant himself does not discuss a rather obvious strategy to seemingly get around moral commands: phrasing one's maxims in such broad or specific ways that they always pass the universalization test.[21] I do not think that Kant means to deny this phenomenon. He is,

---

[20] Likewise, Darwall (1988) emphasizes the importance of the notion of self-deception for any philosophy that focuses on motives and dispositions as opposed to consequences of actions, and his discussion of self-deception focuses on Kant's conception of conscience and opacity of one's own motives. Hill also understands self-deception as a misrepresentation of one's motives or as assuming 'that our motives are good, whatever they are' (Hill 2012: 354). Likewise, Ware (2009) discusses self-deception in the context of opacity of motives. In his recent book he stresses that the 'tendency to deceive ourselves' is the tendency 'to construe our intentions in a flattering or praiseworthy light' (Ware 2021: 15), but also concedes that rationalizing can issue in a 'genuine error of deliberation' (26). Indeed, the focus of the debate has recently shifted somewhat away from motives. Moeller (2020: 104), for instance, describes the attempt of deceiving one's own conscience thusly: the internal 'defence advocate might interpret the incentive as mere negligence rather than intentional wrongdoing'. Moeller does not reduce self-deception to the question of whether actions are morally worthy. She is aware that an investigation of my incentives can impact the question of whether what I did should count as a free and intentional action and can be (fully) imputed to me. I think we can and should go even further than this; attempts to excuse myself or advance spurious justifications for my actions do not have to draw on matters of incentives at all. Finally, Allais (2021: 49) acknowledges the pervasiveness of self-deception on Kant's framework in the sense that self-deception does not only pertain to 'particular actions or particular moral requirements in specific circumstances' but rather 'to the rightfulness of our ways of live'. For this purpose, questions about motivation are important but are not the only ones that matter; self-deception takes the form of presenting 'our motives and ourselves to ourselves as better than they are' (46).

[21] That self-deception only concerns the permissibility of specific maxims is, for instance, maintained by Broadie and Pybus (1982).

however, more interested in strategies that go beyond specific actions or maxims and that impact an agent's conception of *core features of morality* (such as purity and strictness), as these strategies undermine an agent's competence to reason about many or all other moral cases.

2.3 Common Human Reason[22]

To understand the role rationalizing plays for Kant, we need to look at the overall aim of Kant's ethics: clarifying, systematizing and vindicating the common rational cognition of duty. Kant believes that agents endowed with common human reason, meaning the capacities and insights all rational human agents share simply insofar as they are rational, do not need any special training or academic education to know what they ought to do. In a footnote at the beginning of the Second Critique (CPrR, V: 8), he claims that he does not aim to introduce a new principle of morality, and he doubts that pre-theoretical reasoning could be 'ignorant' or 'in thoroughgoing error' about duty (CPrR, V: 8). Indeed, philosophical remarks may 'seem superfluous' (CPrR, V: 36.6) as the requirements of morality can be 'seen quite easily and without hesitation by the most common understanding' (36.28–9). It is the threat of rationalizing and the potential corruption of agents' initial grasp of morality that necessitates a philosophical systematization of the common cognition of duty and a role for practical philosophy in moral development. Let us look briefly at this initial grasp of morality to get a sense of the dangers of rationalizing.

The most central moral insight of common human reason is that duty commands unconditionally and has to be obeyed for its own sake.[23] This acknowledgement of the *unconditional authority of morality* becomes most apparent in the Second Critique's Gallows Case.

> But experience also confirms this order of concepts in us. [...] [A]sk him whether, if his prince demanded, on pain of the same immediate execution, that he give false testimony against an honourable man whom the prince would like to destroy under a plausible pretext, he would consider it possible to overcome his love of life, however great it may be. He would perhaps not venture to assert whether he would do it or not, but he must admit without hesitation that it would be possible for him. He judges, therefore, that he can do something because he is aware that he ought to do it and cognizes freedom

---

[22] In other publications, I have expanded on various aspects of common human reason in Kant, specifically: on its methodological significance (Sticker 2016b, 2017a, 2017b); on moral epistemology (Sticker 2015); conscience (Sticker 2016a); and questions of (cultural) plurality of conceptions of morality (Sticker 2021a). The following brings together salient points made in these publications.

[23] See G, IV: 393.5–7, 397.18–19; TP, VIII: 284.30–3; RPT, VIII: 403.23–5; Ped, IX: 493.35–494.4.

within him, which, without the moral law, would have remained unknown to him. (CPrR, V: 30.21–35)

If we present an agent with this Gallows Case, the agent, Kant believes, 'will perhaps not venture to assert' whether he would have the strength to refuse the prince's unjust demand. He will, however, judge 'without hesitation' that it is *possible* to do so, revealing that he believes that he can act in a certain way because he is aware that he ought to. According to Kant, when confronted with cases that require action for the sake of morality and against their self-interest, agents admit that morality compels them differently from and independently of all other incentives. This reveals that they acknowledge the authority of morality.

Moreover, in order to determine what morality demands of them, Kant believes that all rational human agents, including common agents, those lacking academic training and familiarity with philosophical theory and whose under-standing of morality is based on common human reason, can avail themselves of *universalization* tests. Kant even claims that agents 'always actually have before their eyes and use as the standard of judging' (G, IV: 403.36–7) the principle 'never to proceed except in such a way *that I could also will that my maxim should become a universal law*' (G, IV: 402.7–15).[24] However, we will see in Section 5.2 that this strong claim only holds for uncorrupted agents. Be that as it may, the principle of morality is, in a different form, already employed in non-philosophical reasoning, for instance, when agents wonder 'what if everyone did this?', or when they reflect on whether they are consistent in their assessment of self and others, or whether they exempt themselves from moral requirements they expect others to follow.[25] However, common agents do not think of these ways of reasoning 'as separated [. . .] in a universal form' (G, IV: 403.36; see CPrR, V: 155.16) or in the guise of a philosophical formula, such as the Formula of Universal Law. Their grasp of moral principles is obscure.[26] They can reason about and correctly assess concrete moral cases

---

[24] See also CPrR, V: 69.25–70.4. I develop the notion of pre-theoretical universalization tests in Sticker (2015: sec. 2).

[25] See Piper (2012: 246), Scanlon (2011: 122) and Wood (1999: 108–9) for versions of the universalization procedure along those intuitive lines. See also Sidgwick (1907: book III, chapter 1, sec. 3), who agrees with Kant that universality is of utmost importance for any conscientious person as a subjective test of rightness; if we do not want others to act as we do, our action cannot be permissible. This, however, is a merely negative criterion and does not establish that an action is permissible. I cannot here critically discuss these and other well-known problems for Kantian universalizability. See instead Freyenhagen (2011) and Allison (2011: ch. 7) for overviews. I should also point out that Kant acknowledges a second moral criterion to be found in ordinary moral reasoning (see below).

[26] There is an 'obscurely represented metaphysics, which inheres within every human's rational propensity' (MM, VI: 376.25–6; see also MM, VI: 216.33–4).

but without understanding underlying abstract structures and without knowing the source of morality.

Furthermore, Kant claims that rational human beings are aware that '*a rational nature exists as an end in itself.* That is how a human being by necessity represents his own existence' (G, IV: 429.2–4). Human beings think of their own existence as well as of the existence of other rational creatures as ends in themselves. This imposes constraints on their actions. Kant's Formula of Humanity systematizes how humans understand themselves and others as rational beings who are owed treatment different from non-rational entities. Given that there is more than one way for agents to cognize their duty (universality and the special standing of rational agents), it is a central task of the critical philosopher to construct a theory that accommodates different pre-theoretical ways to cognize duty and that shows how they can be part of an ethical system ultimately grounded in autonomy.[27]

At the end of *Groundwork* I, Kant wonders whether practical philosophy is necessary at all (G, IV: 404.28–30; see also CPrR, V: 36.7–8). After all, a common agent, even without any practical philosophy, 'stands just as good a chance of hitting the mark as a philosopher can ever expect; indeed is almost more sure in this than even the latter' (G, IV: 404.22–5). A philosopher, by contrast, 'can easily confuse' reasoning 'with a host of alien and irrelevant considerations and deflect it from the straight course' (404.27–8). In the penultimate paragraph of *Groundwork* I (G, IV: 404.1–405.19), Kant explains why a systematization and vindication of the common or pre-theoretical way of reasoning is necessary; common agents are caught in a '*natural dialectic*' (G, IV: 405.13) and they are 'easily seduced' (G, IV: 405.1) to prioritize happiness over duty. Kant believes that 'morals themselves remain subject to all sorts of corruption as long as we lack that guideline [*Leitfaden*] and supreme norm by which to judge them correctly'.[28] This guideline has to come from critical practical philosophy. The practical concern to avoid corruption motivates Kant's transition from common rational cognition of duty to a philosophical system grounded in a pure and rational principle (G, IV: 406.2–4).[29]

---

[27] Kant famously maintains that all Categorical Imperative formulations are 'formulae of the selfsame law' (G, IV: 436.8–9). This, however, is controversial. See Kerstein (2002) and Formosa (2017: ch. 1) for sceptical takes on this equivalence claim. I cannot discuss this here. See instead Wood (2017).

[28] G, IV: 390.2–3; see also G, IV: 405.29–30; CPrR, V: 141.29–31, 163.27–35. Gregor (1996: 45) translates *Leitfaden* as 'clue'. Kant then seems to say that without a philosophical investigation we have *no idea* (no clue) about morality – a claim that would be in tension with his claims about common human reason and common agents.

[29] Likewise, Kant's warning against the rationalized eudaemonist attack on the purity of morality appears in the context of motivating the *Doctrine of Virtue* (MM, VI: 371.13–378.31; see also Section 3.2).

Kant's assumption that there are moral insights that all rational humans share reflects an 'egalitarian ideal of enlightenment' (Ameriks 2000: 102), namely that 'what is expected of, and most significant about, human beings must be in principle equally accessible to all and should not depend on the accident of particular external conditions' (228).[30] All rational agents are, at bottom, committed to the same conception of morality, since morality is grounded in their shared rational nature.

Kant's assumption raises at least two problems. First, Kant cannot simply concede that rational agents, if they rationalize too thoroughly, lose their grasp of the moral law entirely and need external help from an ethical expert. This would constitute a form of elitism that Kant is sceptical of. Instead, Kant must explain how practical philosophy can remedy forms of irrationality that can be very serious but that still do not completely undermine an agent's capacity to obtain correct moral insights and do the right thing. According to Kant, even corrupted agents still have what it takes to be regarded as moral agents and as responsible for their actions and their rationalizing.

Second, as a matter of fact, agents frequently do exhibit forms of ethical reasoning, such as consequence-driven evaluations, that seemingly contradict Kant's conception of pre-theorical rational cognition. Kant must therefore provide a plausible account for how it is possible that agents adopt views about morality that deviate from what they are committed to qua rational agents. Karl Ameriks (2000: 150) provocatively claims that Kant has to engage:

> in all sorts of quasi-religious considerations about radical evil and techniques of self-delusion to try to explain how so many people manage to hide from themselves the basic claims of morality that [Kant] believes are as clear in themselves as are the basic claims of our theoretical common sense.

In contrast to Ameriks, I do not regard Kant's discussions of 'self-delusion' as a weakness of his account, but rather as aiming to capture important elements of the psychology of fallible humans. Kant's conception of rationalizing and corruption, if convincing, allows him to reconcile forms of moral error with his (at times highly idealized) description of the insights and capacities even of common agents.

3 Rationalizing and the Natural Dialectic

3.1 The Natural Dialectic

Kant introduces rationalizing in the dense penultimate paragraph of *Groundwork* I.

---

[30] This insight is, as Kant himself acknowledges, inspired by Rousseau (RO, XX: 44.8–16). See Callanan (2019) for a more detailed discussion of Rousseau's influence on Kant.

Innocence is a glorious [1] thing, but then again it is very sad that it is so hard to preserve and so **easily seduced [2]**. Because of this even wisdom – which otherwise probably consists more in behaviour than in knowledge – yet needs science too, not in order to learn from it, but to obtain access and durability for its prescription. The human being feels within himself **a powerful counterweight to all the commands of duty [3]** – which reason represents to him as so worthy of the highest respect – in his needs and inclinations, **the entire satisfaction of which he sums up under the name of happiness [4]**. Now reason issues its prescriptions **unrelentingly, yet without promising anything to the inclinations [5]**, and hence, as it were, **with reproach and disrespect for those claims [6]**, which are so **vehement and yet seem so reasonable (and will not be eliminated by any command) [7]**. But from this there arises a *natural dialectic* **[8]**, i.e., **a propensity to rationalize against those strict laws of duty [9]**, and **to cast doubt on their validity [10]**, or at least their **purity [11]** and **strictness [12]**, and, where possible, to **make them better suited to our wishes and inclinations [13]**, i.e., **fundamentally to corrupt them and deprive them of their entire dignity [14]**, something that in the end even common practical reason cannot endorse. (G, IV: 404.37–405.19)[31]

Common agents, agents whose understanding of morality is based on their common human reason alone, are in a state of 'innocence' [1] and 'fortunate simplicity' (G, IV: 404.34). They understand what matters morally (universality and humanity) and that morality is of supreme authority. However, their grasp of morality is obscure. They lack a reflected understanding of it that would allow them to see through spurious justifications for immoral actions. Innocence is therefore difficult to preserve and common agents are 'easily seduced' [2]. Seduction here indicates that typically an agent is not forced by their inclinations to act against their better judgement, though we will see in Section 5.2 that weakness of will plays a role in the story of corruption. When inclinations present an impermissible course of action as attractive, an agent acquiesces and alters their judgement. The sources of seduction are an agent's needs and inclinations, the satisfaction of which is summed up 'under the name of happiness' [4]. The grip of inclinations will 'not be eliminated by any command' [7]. An agent can never switch off the appeal of objects that promise happiness.[32] Inclinations thus constitute 'a powerful counterweight to all the commands of

---

[31] In Sticker (2016a: 89–91), I present a close reading of this passage specifically pertaining to our understanding of the role of conscience in Kant. The following greatly expands on this and, among other things, clarifies what it means to disregarded purity and strictness in moral reasoning, how these failures differ from each other but also feed into each other and how rationalizing relates to excuses and (pseudo-)justifications.

[32] See also G, IV: 415.28–33; G, IV: 418.1–4; Rel, VI: 45.25–7; TP, VIII: 278.15–21.

duty' [3], and these commands in turn are issued 'without promising anything to the inclinations' [5].[33]

The tension between unconditional commands of duty and personal happiness gives rise to a *'natural dialectic'* [8]. This dialectic is *natural* in the sense that it is rooted in the tension between our rational and our sensuous nature. In contrast to the *Groundwork*, dialectic in the First Critique appears in the form of antinomies constituted by mutually exclusive *propositions* that both rest on a false assumption, namely on transcendental realism (A/B: 502/530).[34] In the *Groundwork*, the tension is not one between propositions, a thesis and an antithesis, but between different determining grounds of an agent's will (happiness and morality), or between their natures in which these determining grounds originate. Kant tries to frame this as a propositional contradiction when he speaks of the contradictory 'claims' [*Ansprüche*] of happiness and morality ([6]; see also G, IV: 405.28). The foundation of the *Groundwork*'s dialectic, however, is not a false philosophical assumption, but the double nature of human beings. The *Groundwork*'s natural dialectic should therefore rather be called a 'natural dialectical tension (between duty and happiness)' to avoid confusion with a dialectic in the terminological sense used in the Critiques.[35]

According to the *Groundwork*, the natural dialectical tension is identical to – Kant uses the strong 'i.e.' [*d.i.*] [9], 'this is', to characterize the relation – 'a propensity to rationalize against those strict laws of duty' [9].[36] Rationalizing

---

[33] See also CPrR, V: 128.16–19; Rel, VI: 49.17; Eth-M2, XXIX: 624.19–20. However, we will see below (Section 4.3) that pure practical reason does affect personal happiness.

[34] In the Third Critique, Kant claims that the antinomy of the teleological power of judgement gives rise to a 'natural dialectic', which deserves its name because the 'necessary maxims of the reflexive capacity of judgement' in which the antinomy is grounded are themselves grounded in the nature of our faculty of cognition (CJ, V: 386.4–10). 'Natural' here means that something is necessary for creatures with our type of cognitive capacities. This is similar to the sense in which a dialectic is necessary in our theoretical reasoning (see A/B: 297–8/354–5; P, IV: 329.14–24, 341fn., 347.24, 353.16–31; CPrR, V: 108.3–12).

[35] Guyer (2003: 30) and Zhouhuang (2016: 68–9) read the natural dialectical tension as akin to the Second Critique's dialectic, and Callanan (2019: sec. 6) stresses that the natural dialectic is a genuine dialectic since two rational faculties (pure practical and empirical practical reason), both operating as they should, create conflicting claims. Allison (2011: 144–5), by contrast, stresses the difference between the dialectics in the *Groundwork* and the Critiques. He even claims that Kant's *Groundwork* I conclusion that a critique of reason is called for as a response to the natural dialectic is 'highly artificial' (144). I believe that Allison is right to stress the difference between the dialectical tension and a proper dialectic. Yet, even though not a proper dialectic, the dialectical tension is central for understanding the need for practical philosophy.

[36] In the Third Critique, by contrast, Kant explains rationalizing as the act of claiming universality for one's judgements, which can lead to a dialectic (CJ, V: 337.5–8; see Section 2.1). Rationalizing here precedes the dialectic. According to the *Groundwork*, the natural dialectic is a propensity to rationalize and thus precedes rationalizing. This is the same as in the First Critique, where rationalizing is presented as an exercise of rational capacities without awareness of their dialectical nature, resulting in antinomical claims (A/B: 422/450; see also A/B: 63/87–8, 421/448–9). The dialectic here precedes rationalizing or is a condition thereof.

ultimately amounts to challenging the 'validity' [10] of the moral law. This, however, does not mean that a rationalizer renounces commitment to morality. Rationalizing only makes sense for agents committed to morality.[37] Rationalizers 'transform' (G, IV: 424.31) their conception of morality into one which better suits their 'wishes and inclinations' [13]. Any such modification, Kant fears, would fundamentally 'corrupt' [14] the strict laws of duty, 'and deprive them of their entire dignity' [14]. Kant here once more uses the strong 'i.e.' [*d.i.*], this time to indicate the relation between transforming one's conception of morality and corruption [14]. He thinks that this transformation is not merely an activity that *can* result in corruption, but corruption itself.

A modified conception of morality conditions obedience to the moral law on non-moral factors, such as one's own and others' inclinations and personal ends, though the moral law is still a point of reference for the rationalizer. Rationalizing alters the way an agent thinks about morality and assesses herself. Even if a rationalizer acts for the sake of the (supposedly) moral principles that she accepts, these principles themselves might be too different from the moral law to confer moral worth on actions. Corruption is thus a twofold problem. First, false principles might lead an agent to *judge incorrectly*. Second, actions no longer express *unconditional commitment to duty*.[38]

I should flag already that the way Kant describes the mechanism of rationalizing – transforming one's conception of morality into one that is more in line with one's pursuit of personal happiness, without renouncing morality altogether – can only explain why agents would buy into overly *lenient* moral theories. There is a converse excess, though: adopting an overly rigorous and excessively demanding theory. Rationalizing seems unable to help us

---

[37] See Section 4.3, as well as G, IV: 424.36–7; CPrR, V: 152.10–11; MM, VI: 321.38–9; Eth-M2, XXIX: 609.34–6, 629.2–5; Shell (2009:177); Grenberg (2010: 158). Most recently, Callanan (2019: 7) has emphasized that 'Kant's account of the natural dialectic – and with it the justification for moral philosophy itself – is targeted on the problem of moral corruption rather than moral scepticism. Kant views this type of morally unresponsive attitude as pernicious just because it allows one to challenge the reality of morality without realizing that one is doing so. The effect is arguably more pernicious than moral scepticism just because the degradation of our moral commitments is undergone while we nevertheless pay lip service to the idea of respecting the demands of morality. Crucially perhaps, moral corruption is also plausibly a far more common real-world phenomenon than that of decrying morality per se.' I think this is correct. Corruption requires that agents still buy into morality, and it thus cannot be a form of complete scepticism. Callanan is also right that few agents are complete sceptics about morality (especially when their own rights and moral status are concerned). However, many agents are sometimes sceptics about central aspects of morality, such as strictness and purity, namely when the commands of duty turn out to be particularly burdensome on them. This selective form of scepticism qualifies as rationalizing.

[38] The distinction between two different problems posed by corruption was one of the main upshots of Sticker (2016a: sec. 1.2).

understand why agents would ever come to accept such a theory. I will come back to this in Section 6.

3.2 Purity and Strictness

Rationalizing divides into two main strategies: casting doubt on the purity [11] and strictness [12] of duty.

(i) *Purity* represents the idea that agents are to abstract from their personal ends and inclinations when reasoning about what their duty is and when acting on the outcome of their moral reasoning.[39] Purity first requires that nothing empirical – that is, inclinations, an agent's personal ends, consequences of actions and so on – functions as *criteria* for moral evaluation. This is the *cognitive* component. Second, purity requires that obligatory actions and omissions are *motivated* by respect for the moral law, or at least that an agent commits themselves to duty unconditionally.[40] The cognitive and motivational components are closely related, since agents treating something empirical as a criterion for moral evaluation will likely perform actions motivated by this empirical concern. An agent who assigns moral significance to their own inclinations will likely be motivated by these inclinations rather than by the moral law.[41]

In the preface to the *Doctrine of Virtue*, Kant provides a detailed example for a case of rationalizing against the purity of morality. After having done his duty, Kant explains, an agent can find himself in a state 'that could well be called happiness' (MM, VI: 377.21–2).[42] This experience can be misinterpreted as support for eudaemonism. Eudaemonism, according to Kant, is the position that

---

[39] Sensitivity to one's own and to others' inclinations can be relevant and permissible for the application of imperfect duties to concrete cases (G, IV: 411.8–412.14; CPrR, V: 8.15–24; MM, VI: 216.28–217.27; Eth-M1, XXVII: 1398.21–4; Eth-M2, XXIX: 599.11–15). See Seymour Fahmy (2019: sec. 4), who argues that the application of obligatory ends will frequently have to be informed by prudential considerations. Moreover, Kant indicates that pursuing personal happiness is rational and permissible as long as it does not conflict with duty (CPrR, V: 93.11–15; see also TP, VIII: 283.6–10).

[40] I want to remain neutral concerning the difficult question of whether Kant thinks that every individual moral action must be motivated by respect, or whether agents should commit themselves steadfastly to duty and act in the light of this commitment without respect having to function as the effective motive for every individual moral action. See Ameriks (2003: ch. 7) for discussion.

[41] This is a sign of insufficient commitment to duty, even if we think that not every individual action must be motivated by respect. After all, holding oneself justified before the moral law regardless of motives is 'deceit of the human heart' (Rel, VI: 38.7–8). See also CPrR, V: 151.13–152.18; Rel, VI: 69–70fn.; Eth-K: 86.

[42] Kant here refers to *moral* pleasure, which results from obeying the moral law (MM, VI: 378.8–14; RPT, VIII: 395–6fn.). See also Rel, VI: 67.17–68.3; MM, VI: 211.10–18, 391.16–25; P-M, XXIII: 373.6–374.7; Eth-V, XXVII: 497.35–498.14. Most recently, Cohen (2020: 451) has emphasized the 'distinctly moral' dimensions of this feeling.

every action, including moral action, requires the prospect of reward or punishment.[43] Agents might interpret happiness resulting from moral actions as a necessary driving force of these actions and even convince themselves that duty is only a *means* to achieve happiness.

According to eudaemonism, we can 'recognize' that something is our duty only if we 'can count on gaining happiness by doing it' (MM, VI: 377.21–378.5). A eudaemonist in this sense is still committed to obeying moral commands, but only because they see this as the best way to pursue happiness. In fact, for them it is the hallmark of duty that it yields happiness. Kant calls the eudaemonist's inference from the existence of happiness that succeeds moral actions to the thesis that personal happiness is the goal of morality 'rationalizing' (MM, VI: 378.1) a 'rationalizing trifling' (TP, VIII: 284.5) and 'as it were, [. . .] an optical illusion in the self-consciousness of what one *does* as distinguished from what one *feels* – an illusion that even the most practiced cannot altogether avoid' (CPrR, V: 116.22–5).[44]

Eudaemonism is the '*euthanasia* (the gentle death) of all morals' (MM, VI: 378.18; see also CPrR, V: 88.21–89.8). Interestingly, Kant here translates '*euthanasia*', which more literally means 'good death', as 'gentle' or 'easy' [*sanft*] death. Corruption does not occur as an abrupt and voluntary rupture with the authority of the moral law. It is the result of a slow and subtle process. An agent deems herself fully committed to morality throughout this process but, in the end, true morality has (almost fully) passed away without the agent noticing. In the example presented by Kant, it is the satisfaction that a moral agent feels upon believing to have done the right thing that subsequently becomes material for rationalizing. Perversely, it seems that particularly those agents are prone to rationalizing who greatly value morality and for whom moral action is a source of personal fulfilment, since these agents cannot face the prospect of failing to live up to moral commands. I will discuss this in more detail in the next section.

(ii) *Strictness* represents the idea that (perfect) duties never admit of exceptions.[45] Agents disregard this requirement when they reason as if the

---

[43] 'Now the *eudaemonist* says: this delight, this happiness is really his motive for acting virtuously. The concept of duty does not determine his will *directly*, he is moved to do his duty only *by means of* the happiness he anticipates' (MM, VI: 377.24–7).

[44] The optical illusion, a metaphor taken from the realm of perception, is supposed to indicate that an agent takes something merely subjective (the way it appears to them) to be objective (the way it is for everyone). Kant also calls this illusion 'an error of subreption (*vitium subreptionis*)' (CPrR, V: 116.21–2), which he elsewhere explains as confusing the intellectual or objective with the sensuous or subjective (Ref, XV: 93.14–16, 94.19–22; LB-Prog, XX: 349.3–16). A *vitium subreptionis praticum* specifically is when one mistakes actions from sensuous motives for actions from principles (Ref, XV: 454.22–4).

[45] I take it that Kant's main focus here is *perfect* duties. For recent discussion of the latitude of imperfect duties, see Timmermann (2018) and van Ackeren and Sticker (2018). Imperfect duties are strict in the sense that at least *adopting* obligatory ends is not optional.

normative force of moral commands can be outweighed by non-moral factors, or as if duty is only to be obeyed if it falls below a certain threshold of sacrifice. For these agents the moral law is transformed into a principle of merely general validity, that is, one which admits of exceptions (G, IV: 424.25–33).[46]

Kant draws examples for rationalizing against strictness mainly from the social sphere, more specifically from the '*religion of rogation* (of mere cult)' (Rel, VI: 51.27), or '*fetish-faith*' (Rel, VI: 193.21; see also Eth-V, XXVII: 729.16).[47] Praying and attending church, as well as rituals such as baptism, communion, public sacrifice, penance, castigation, pilgrimage and so on, are supposed to function as a 'shortcut' or 'hidden path' [*Schleichweg*][48] (Rel, VI: 193.28) to divine grace (Rel, VI: 192.1–202.5).[49] According to Kant, '[t]he more useless such self-inflicted torments are, the less aimed at universal moral improvement of the human being, the holier they seem to be' (Rel, VI: 169.17–19; see also Eth-K: 153).[50] Performing supposedly 'holy' actions commended by religious authorities and in plain sight of others can make an agent feel more moral than actually performing actions of genuine moral worth, especially if they receive public recognition for it. Moreover, the teachings and practices of the cult suggest to agents that God can make them better human beings without active contribution on their end (Rel, VI: 51.22–37). This can easily become material for rationalizing as it seemingly allows agents to shift responsibility for their moral improvement away from them.

An even more direct example of disregarding strictness is the notion of a *last confession*, which suggests that a moral disposition does not require exceptionless adherence to duty. Instead, one can confess one's sins at the last possible moment to escape eternal punishment (Eth-K: 192–3; see also Rel, VI: 77.26–78.2). Kant expresses similar concerns regarding the proverb 'All is well that ends well' (Rel, VI: 70fn., 77.26–78.2), which suggests that only the last disposition of an agent matters for the assessment of her entire life.

---

[46] For Kant's recurring warnings against making exceptions, see also G, IV: 424.15–37; Rel, VI: 32.13; MM, VI: 321.27–322.21; Eth-M2, XXIX: 6292–5. See Sensen (2014) for development of this theme.

[47] The cult or 'counterfeit service (*cultus spurious*)' (Rel, VI: 153.18–19), a 'system of religious make-up' [*Religionsschminke*] (Eth-K: 157), is most extensively discussed throughout the *Religion* and in Eth-K: 115–65; P-F, XXIII: 445.21–446.27; Eth-V, XXVII: 729.16–732.6.

[48] Wood and Di Giovanni (1998: 185) translate *Schleichweg* as 'escape route'. This makes it sound as if agents want to *escape* morality, when, in fact, they are looking for an easier way to *satisfy* moral commands.

[49] See also Rel, VI: 168.8–170.11; MM, VI: 430.19–26; MPT, VIII: 265.28–266.5, 200.11–34; Eth-K: 154–7.

[50] Kant also worries that '*penance* [. . .] which is cheerless, gloomy and sullen, makes virtue itself hated and drives adherents away from it' (MM, VI: 485.28–9).

The common element of all forms of rationalizing against strictness is that an agent is aware that what they do is against duty or at least morally questionable, but they also believe that they can wash away the stain on their character or that God can rid them of sin. They feel excused in their wrongdoings. Kant does not say whether such an agent explicitly believes that morality admits of exceptions or merely reasons about morality as if this were so. I think both can be the case. Rationalizers can explicitly endorse overly lenient conceptions of morality, according to which laxness and also impurity are features of moral principles.[51] Presumably, an agent who explicitly believes that morality admits of exceptions is more corrupted than an agent who merely reasons as if this were the case. The latter might still acknowledge their mistakes once they clearly understand that their reasoning conflicts with one of the central tenets of morality, whereas the former has given up on this tenet.

Rationalizers always retain a commitment to morality, but this commitment is no longer unconditional. Either they are unconditionally committed to an impure principle, which combines elements of morality and inclinations (*no-purity*), or they are committed conditionally to a pure principle, thinking that (or reasoning as if) there can be exceptions and excuses to a law that abstracts from all inclinations (*no-strictness*). In the case of no-purity, impure elements are part of the supposedly moral principle itself. This is particularly dangerous, since even when agents do what they think is morally required, they act from a principle that gives undue weight to their own inclinations in the sense that supposed moral commands are (partly) determined by inclinations or personal ends. In the case of no-strictness, agents can still act from a pure principle but their obedience to duty is conditioned on non-moral factors, and their disposition not entirely moral (see also Sticker 2016a: 90–1). Moreover, agents can even think of moral principles as sensitive to their inclinations (no-purity), and as also admitting of exceptions (no-strictness). They are then conditionally committed to an impure principle. They believe that morality is (partly or entirely) determined by their inclinations and personal ends, and if their conception of morality nonetheless requires them to do something they find inconvenient, they might also think it legitimate to make an exception to their already lenient principle(s). An important difference between purity and strictness is that an agent who has abandoned purity believes that they are morally justified in what they are doing, because impure elements supposedly affect questions of moral permissibility. An agent who has abandoned strictness, by contrast, merely assumes that there are grounds of excuses for not heeding the pure

---

[51] For instance, an agent who levels an overdemandingness objection against a moral theory explicitly takes issue with the purity of morality. They think that a moral theory is deficient if it does not leave enough room for their personal ends (see Section 6).

commands of morality. The latter agent will still 'at the same time detest his transgression' (MM, VI: 321.38) at least to some extent, since they are aware that their actions lack full moral justification.

For the ensuing discussion it will be important to distinguish explicitly between justifications and excuses. An agent is morally *justified* when they did what duty commanded or permitted them to do. An agent is *excused* when they acknowledge that one of their actions was not (fully) morally justified, but their responsibility is mitigated.[52] Excuses, in turn, can represent genuinely relevant factors that make a wrongdoing less imputable, such as that an agent faced extraordinary obstacles (MM, VI: 228.11–22). They can also be based on flimsy grounds and merely serve to make the agent feel better about themselves or to deceive others. It is part of our ordinary conception of excuses that they can genuinely exculpate, as well as be mere attempts to make oneself look better. In the latter case, we might say something like 'You are just making excuses', which, in a sense, is odd, given that excuses can have a legitimate impact on moral assessment. Kant is sceptical even of excuses that actually mitigate responsibility, because he worries that once we take ourselves to be excused, we might also appeal to the excuse in ex ante reasoning about what duty requires. This would be incompatible with the purity of duty as it would introduce non-moral concerns into moral deliberation (see Section 5 for more).

In what follows, three points will become important. First, for Kant, rationalizing primarily interferes with *self*-assessment. The rationalizer presents their own, past or intended, actions as better than they are and they do so to *themselves*.[53] Self-assessment is usually concerned with justifications, and excuses are typically something we give to *others*. It is possible, though, that upon realizing that I did something wrong, I wonder whether there is anything to excuse my action to myself. In addition, while it is normal to wonder about the justifiability of one's actions retrospectively as well as prospectively, excuses are usually sought only in retrospect. There is something odd about an agent who knows that their intended action is morally unjustified, but nonetheless looks for ex ante excuses. It rather seems that this agent lowered the bar for what counts as a justification.[54]

---

[52] My discussion of the differences between justifications and excuses has benefited much from Baron (2005, 2007), and I am grateful to Marcia Baron, Stefano Lo Re and Claudia Blöser for discussion.

[53] However, rationalizing also can extend to deception of others (see Section 5).

[54] Schapiro (2006: 41), by contrast, proposes that we understand an excuse as 'a special case of justification, one in which the agent is aware of having to act in what she conceives of as a marginal case'. Excuses here can also be prospective. However, Shapiro admits that 'the notion of an excuse is also, and perhaps more commonly, used in connection with retrospective judgments of responsibility'.

Second, we will see (Section 4.3) that the goal of rationalizing is to avoid pangs of conscience and to make ourselves believe that we deserve happiness. For these purposes, justifications are more potent than excuses. After all, the former suggest that the agent does not need to improve at all, whereas the latter imply an admission of behaviour that was, at least, non-ideal. However, particularly in early stages of corruption, when the agent still has a relatively clear grasp of right and wrong, it might well be the case that the only venue of rationalizing open to them is to acknowledge that they did wrong and to find or invent an excuse.

Third, it becomes apparent in some of the strategies of rationalizing discussed by Kant that there is more to rationalizing than misrepresenting the *strength or source of one's motives*, such as the last confession and appeal to religious authorities. Here rationalizers aim to make room for exceptions to duty and rationalizing might even result in an altered understanding of what matters for moral deliberation. Furthermore, rationalizing is more than the attempt to deceive oneself about the moral permissibility of *specific maxims or actions*. Kant's discussion of rationalizing at the end of *Groundwork* I as well as many of his examples are focused on strategies that transform one's conception of morality into one which better suits one's inclinations, and undermine an agent's competence to reason about many, maybe all, morally relevant cases.

4 The Cunning of (Empirical Practical) Reason

I will now look at the structures that make rationalizing possible. I first explain why the framework Kant himself suggests as a blueprint for understanding self-deception, the inner lie and the distinction between *homo noumenon* and *homo phaenomenon*, is inadequate for understanding rationalizing (Section 4.1). I then elaborate on a better framework that draws on the distinction between different aspects of reason (Sections 4.2–5). My investigation will reveal how a number of rational faculties contribute to rationalizing. Clarifying the exact nature of these contributions will help us understand how rationalizing can be a rational, yet flawed, activity.

4.1 The Internal Lie

Kant himself most explicitly elaborates on the metaphysical and psychological conditions of self-deception in the *Doctrine of Virtue*, §9. According to Kant, lies can be 'external' and intended to deceive others, or 'internal' and intended to deceive oneself (MM, VI: 429.13–14). Kant stresses that self-deception happens 'on purpose' (MM, VI: 430.12–13) and 'deserves the strongest censure' (MM, VI: 430.35–6). However, to 'intentionally deceive oneself seems to contain a contradiction' (MM, VI: 429.12–13). Deceptive strategies normally cannot be employed against someone who knows about the deceptive intention. Nonetheless, self-deception seems to require just this. This problem is sometimes called the 'Paradox of Strategy'.[55] As a response to this paradox some philosophers suggest a *mental partitioning* model; one cognitive system of an agent employs a deceptive strategy against another system of the same agent and unbeknownst to that latter system, much like when one agent deceives another.[56]

Kant acknowledges that his model rests on a partitioning. Internal lies are difficult to explain, 'because a second person is required' (MM, VI: 430.11; see also Ref, XVII: 320.16–19). He suggests that the required partitioning is the distinction between 'the human being as a moral being (*homo noumenon*)' and 'as a natural being (*homo phaenomenon*)' (MM, VI: 430.14–15). Kant emphasizes that this distinction is made 'in a practical respect' (MM, VI: 439.31). It is one between different ways of regarding 'the same human being' (MM, VI: 418.17; see also MM, VI: 239.27–8).[57]

While Kant frequently draws on this distinction to explain duties to self (MM, VI: 418.5–23; Eth-V, XXVII: 539.1–16, 579.8–23), as a framework to explain self-deception the distinction is unconvincing. Kant says that the *homo noumenon* 'cannot use himself as a natural being (*homo phaenomenon*) as a mere means (a speaking machine)' (M, IV: 430.13–16). This is puzzling as the *homo noumenon* cannot do anything immoral anyway, since it is our 'legislating reason' (MM, VI: 335.19; see also MM, VI: 439fn.34; P-M, XXIII: 398.11–12). It is thus simply a truism, not a normative constraint, that the *homo noumenon* cannot use the *homo phaenomenon* for immoral purposes. If anything, Kant here claims that all self-deception is impossible. Moreover, even if the *homo noumenon* could violate duty, it is difficult to see how Kant's warning of using the *homo phenomenon* as a mere *means* can capture the phenomenon of *self*-deception. The metaphor of a 'speaking machine' [*Sprachmaschine*] (MM, VI: 430.16) rather sounds as if the *homo phaenomenon* communicates in a deceptive way with *other agents*.[58]

---

[55] See, for instance, Mele (1987: ch. 10).   [56] See, for instance, Sorensen (1985).

[57] See also MM, VI: 239.26, 418.5, 434.32; Eth-V, XXVII: 504.29, 505.5–39, 510.5, 579.17–18. Sensen (2013: 269) emphasizes that the *homo noumenon* 'is not an obscure metaphysical being, but what a human being conceives himself to be according to the Categorical Imperative'.

[58] Like me, Papish (2018: ch. 3) believes that the internal lie is not a good way to understand self-deception. Her main argument is that Kant here models self-deception too much on deception of others and misses the specific epistemic dimensions of self-deception, such as that it involves disregard for evidence. Bacin (2013: 251–2) argues that 'internal lie' is, in fact, Kant's term for a lie to *others* that makes an agent contemptible in her own eyes. This chimes better with the framework Kant uses to explain this transgression than the standard interpretation, according to

It is important to bear in mind that Kant's discussion of the internal lie is part of his discussion of perfect duties to *self*. Kant might believe that he can account for self-deception within the framework of the two *homines*, since they are central for explaining the possibility of duties to self. From being able to explain how one can put oneself under obligation at all, however, it does not follow that the *homines* must be part of an account of how specific violations of duties to self are possible. Kant has, I think, more promising ways to account for the divisions self-deception about morality presupposes. The most basic of these divisions is between a sensuous and a rational nature (see Section 3.1). This division is different from the one between the *homines*, since sensuous nature is, unlike the *homo phaenomenon*, without reason.[59] In fact, Kant characterizes the *homo phaenomenon* in MM, VI: 430.15 as a 'physical being', without mentioning any rational capacities. He might have an agent's sensuous nature in mind here, rather than what he elsewhere calls the *homo phaenomenon*, a 'sensible being endowed with reason' but lacking *pure* practical reason (MM, VI: 439.30–1; see also MM, VI: 418.14–17).

Having a sensuous and a rational nature, however, only accounts for the dialectical *tension* between duty and happiness. It does not yet explain how it is possible for an agent to resolve this tension via rationalizing. In the *Groundwork*, Kant stresses that the natural dialectic unfolds when common practical reason 'cultivates itself' (G, VI: 405.31). Rationalizing is committed by the 'thoughtful man' (MM, VI: 377.18; see also CB, VIII: 120.28–121.1). Rationalizing is impossible without thought and rational capacities and not even a desideratum for an agent who does not care about moral justification. The division we are looking for has to be one *within* our rational capacities.[60]

In what follows, I cannot discuss in detail how Kant distinguishes between the theoretical and practical use or 'application' (G, IV: 391.28) of reason, and between the different criteria that can guide the practical use of reason (morality, prudence, means-ends rationality; see G, IV: 415.6–418.1; CPrR, V: 25.1; Eth-M2, XXIX: 607.1–4). I will focus on those aspects of reason that contribute to rationalizing: theoretical reason (Section 4.2), pure practical reason

---

which the internal lie refers to self-deception (see, e.g., Potter 2002: 386; Wood 2008: 255; Welsch 2019: 50–1; Di Giulio 2020: 249–59).

[59] Sometimes, however, Kant does seem to indicate that all rational capacities except pure practical reason are part of our animal nature (MM, VI: 418.5–23).

[60] In fact, for Kant sensuousness alone is never a sufficient explanation for immoral action (see Rel, VI: 20.35–22.9, 35.17–20, 58.1, 83.19–20; Eth-V, XXVII: 49420–3). In the *Religion*, he argues against the Stoics that the enemy of virtue is not 'unconcealed' inclination (Rel, VI: 57.19–20), but 'rather an invisible enemy, one who hides behind reason and hence [is] all the more dangerous' (Rel, VI: 21–2; see also CPrR, V: 86.28–9). That self-deception is an 'eminently rational activity' is evidence that for Kant evil is not a form of irrationality but a secret league of reason with temptation (Caswell 2006: 645).

(Section 4.3), common human reason (Section 4.4) and empirical practical reason (Section 4.5). In doing so, I will also draw on the existing Kant literature's suggestions concerning which rational faculties enable and even motivate errors and fallacious reasoning. I will assess and synthesize these suggestions into a comprehensive account of the (pseudo-)rationality of rationalizing.

I should note here that while I will discuss how our various rational faculties contribute to rationalizing, this is not meant to let the *agent* off the hook. After all, it is the *agent* who engages in rationalizing. My investigation is intended to explain how it is possible that agents can engage in rationalizing and why they are incentivized to do so, not to shift the blame for rationalizing away from them.

4.2 Theoretical Reason

Henry Allison (2011: 350) believes that 'common human reason for Kant, at least in the practical domain, is not intrinsically problematic, and only becomes a problem when confronted with a challenge from speculation'. Allison is certainly right that Kant is worried about the effect speculation can have on the common rational cognition of morality. After all, this cognition makes tacit metaphysical assumptions, such as that rational human beings are free to do what they acknowledge they ought to do (see the Gallows Case in Section 2.3). Calling these assumptions into question can undermine the effectiveness of moral commands, as an agent might gradually erode their own confidence that they are able to do the right thing. Kant is particularly concerned about denying human freedom and putting human beings in the same category as 'the other living machines' (TPP, VIII: 378.19–33; see also G, IV: 455.28–456.6). Furthermore, agents who cease to believe in God might think that moral actions are ultimately pointless, since there is no higher authority which distributes happiness according to desert. This can discourage them (CJ, V: 452.30–453.5).[61]

These strategies, I believe, capture in particular the ways in which educated people rationalize, since they concern abstract metaphysical questions that agents without academic training or a tendency towards speculation might not worry about. Furthermore, these strategies are dangerous due to their

---

[61] See also the warning against losing moral self-confidence in Eth-K: 96–7, and Kohl (2017a: 664), who points out that '[m]oral despair clearly is a problem in Kant's ethics'. Kant also criticizes philosophical speculations that result in incorrect models of agency (see also Section 5.1). For instance, he criticizes Leibniz's Principle of Sufficient Reason for 'violating both healthy understanding and even morality' (PM, XX: 283.15–16), since, according to this principle, evil is rooted in mere limitations and lack of virtue as opposed to excessive self-love (PM, XX: 282.26–283.22). I am grateful to Desmond Hogan for this reference. See Piper (2012b: 115) for further discussion of rationalizers who attack the theoretical foundations of morality.

indirectness. Rationalizers think that they have left their conception of what ought to be done untouched, and that they only ponder abstract matters. These abstract ponderings can, however, impact their readiness to do the right thing. Moreover, these strategies differ from many other forms of rationalizing in that the initial intention here might be genuinely innocent and even admirable, namely to get to the bottom of fundamental questions. Yet, Kant worries that even metaphysicians who start with the best of intentions might erode their commitment to morality.[62]

Even though speculation and uncritical metaphysics can deliver material for rationalizing, for two reasons it cannot be the case that rational capacities in the practical sphere are problematic *only* because of challenges from speculation. First, theoretical reason itself is neutral concerning the determination of actions and matters of practical justification. These are simply not the kind of questions it engages with (see CPrR, V: 125.31–4). Second, the majority of rationalizing strategies Kant presents are not concerned with metaphysical principles, but, as we saw in Section 3, with excuses, assumptions about responsibility for moral improvement and the role inclinations, other agents and figures of authority play for moral evaluation. Metaphysical assumptions are in the background of some of these strategies, but rationalizing predominately leads to and exhibits *practical* misconceptions.

A noteworthy example for rationalizing in a circumspect way that does not require theoretical sophistication is presented in the Second Critique. Kant observes that there are conversations in 'mixed company' (CPrR, V: 153.13), that is, company not consisting merely of male scholars but also of academically uneducated men and women. These conversations primarily constitute examples for good reasoning. Kant assumes that in a conversation about concrete actions in morally relevant situations participants 'are precise, refined, and subtle in thinking out everything that could lessen or even just make suspect the purity of purpose and consequently the degree of virtue in it' (CPrR, V: 153.27–8). Making supposed examples of virtuous human character 'suspect' (CPrR, V: 153.29) by questioning the purity of motives can be an expression of 'well-meant strictness in determining genuine moral import in accordance with an uncompromising law' (CPrR, V: 154.4–5) and can serve to 'lower self-conceit in moral matters' (CPrR, V: 154.6). However, Kant also worries that in such conversations morality can be 'rationalized away' (*wegvernünfteln*) and virtue presented as an 'empty name' (CPrR, V: 154.3)'.[63] As a result any striving towards virtue would be 'depreciated as

---

[62] I am grateful to Joe Saunders for suggesting this additional point to me.

[63] Ware (2021: 28) argues that it is a major concern for Kant that morality might turn out to be a 'figment of the imagination' (G, IV: 407.17).

vain affectation and delusive self-conceit' (CPrR, V: 154.15–16; see also Eth-K: 132–5). When these conversations go wrong, when they are captured by rationalizing, rationalizers stress the purity of the moral law and the frailty of human nature. The combination of purity and frailty makes it supposedly impossible to fully comply with the moral law, and this is considered an excuse for not even trying to do so (see also RPT, VIII: 379.32–5). Rationalizers can deconstruct supposed examples of moral actions by giving alternative accounts of the actions in terms of self-interest. The result is a sceptical attitude towards those who profess to strive for virtue as well as scepticism towards the very command to strive for virtue itself. This attitude is not based on metaphysical speculation but rather on supposed life experience and cynicism. Moreover, rationalizers here believe themselves to be assisting morality when they reason that the demands of morality must be lowered to ensure that agents are willing to comply at all.[64]

This example demonstrates that even non-philosophers can rationalize in circumspect and indirect ways, though standard forms of rationalizing are more direct. They proceed from an agent's endeavour to excuse a moral mistake or to convince themselves that a concrete action they want to perform is morally permissible. Moreover, once more Kant indicates that certain forms of rationalizing are especially appealing to agents who take morality (including its core features) very seriously. This raises the question of how an agent's regard for duty feeds into the process of rationalizing.

4.3 Pure Practical Reason

In contrast to Allison's focus on speculation, Paul Guyer (2000: 209) claims that 'our practical reason is inherently liable to undermine our common rational cognition of morals by a dialectic that is entirely natural to it'. I think this a correct description of the natural dialectical tension on a very general level. However, 'practical reason' can refer to a number of different aspects of our rational faculties. Let us begin our discussion of practical reason by looking at *pure* practical reason.

Even though Kant seems to suggest that the *homo noumenon* could use the *homo phaenomenon* as a means (see Section 4.1), the deceptive aspect of our reason cannot be pure practical reason, as this is the source of morality. If it were deceptive there would be no right option an agent could deceive themselves about (see explicitly Rel, VI: 35.9–26).

---

[64] Piper (1987: 109) warns that the notion 'that few of us indeed can be morally effective as martyrs' can be deployed to seemingly justify 'the withdrawal of the self into a private domain' in which moral demands 'can be safely disregarded'.

However, pure practical reason does play a role for self-deception, as was already indicated in the case of the eudaemonist who is initially fully committed to morality and for whom moral action is a source of personal fulfilment (see Section 3.2). Moreover, Kant believes that a 'righteous' agent cannot enjoy their life if they are not aware of the 'righteousness' of their actions. Without this awareness moral self-condemnation will 'deprive [them] of all enjoyment of the agreeableness that [their] state might otherwise contain' (CPrR, V: 116.5–10). Kant describes in great length how the capacity to be moral is the source of self-esteem and 'reverence' for one's own existence (CPrR, V: 87.11). Understanding oneself as being able to live up to the commands of the moral law is essential to an agent's conception of themselves as a rational being. A rational agent 'dreads nothing more than to find, on self-examination, that [they are] worthless and contemptible in [their] own eyes' (CPrR, V: 161.20–1).[65]

Kant explicitly claims that '*pain* one feels from the pangs of conscience has a moral source' (MM, VI: 394.3–5), whereas doing the right thing results in '*moral well-being*': being free of the pangs of conscience (MM, VI: 394.1–12). The latter is not '*positive* (joy) but merely *negative* (relief from preceding anxiety)' (MM, VI: 440.31–2). According to Kant's descriptions of the impact of negative outcomes of moral self-assessment, these can affect us in two ways. First, we cannot (fully) enjoy our life if we believe that we do not deserve happiness.[66] Second, we feel direct pain (irrespective of how good our fortune is) from pangs of conscience and loss of self-esteem. In terms of prudence the best an agent can do is to find a way that maximizes their satisfaction of inclinations, while at the same time minimizing pangs of conscience and the feeling of unworthiness, such that on balance the agent is maximally happy. This might sometimes require actions in accordance with duty (if otherwise the pangs of conscience would be too severe), but often the prudent course of action is to satisfy one's inclinations and to try to find excuses and apparent justifications.

I suggest that we understand agents' concern for moral justifications and excuses as expressions of a *rational interest in being morally justified*.[67] I use

---

[65] See also G, IV: 426.6; CPrR, V: 37.14–21, 88.3–15; Eth-V, XXVII: 575.34–6.

[66] Note that in the Second Critique Kant explicitly speaks of 'righteous' [*rechtschaffen*] agents, not of *virtuous* ones. This suggests that only violating *perfect* duties of right undermines our worthiness to be happy (CPrR, V: 116.5–10). Presumably, agents do not have to know that they are *completely* moral to enjoy their lives. After all, they can never be certain of this (see below in this section). It is sufficient if agents, after ample self-scrutiny, become convinced that their character is not so bad that an impartial observer would disapprove of their happiness (see G, IV: 393.19–24). I elaborate in more detail on how self-assessment can impact agents in Sticker (2021b: sec. 3).

[67] One might think that the interest should rather be understood as *believing* oneself to be morally justified. This is, however, not how the agent themselves thinks of their interest. Agents can only hope to trick their better selves if they think that they have a genuine justification.

'interest' here in the Kantian sense as 'the combination of the pleasure with the faculty of desire [...] so far as this connection is judged through the understanding to be valid according to a universal rule (if only for the subject)' (MM, VI: 212.23–5). Interest in this sense always ultimately aims at pleasure. Unlike a mere desire or inclination, interest is principle-guided and reflected, and can have a source in pure practical reason (G, IV: 413–14fn., 459–60fn.). Respect for the moral law is a '*moral interest*' (CPrR, V: 79.23), which functions as an incentive for moral actions. There are rational interests other than respect.[68] One such interest could be the rational interest in being morally justified. This interest is rooted in an agent's acknowledgement of the authority of duty and pushes them to devise excuses and pseudo-justifications to avoid pain that they would not feel were it not for the effect of pure practical reason on them.[69]

Thinking of *pure* practical reason as part of the process of rationalizing is certainly unorthodox, as Kant is usually unambivalently positive about this part of our rational nature. For instance, he stresses that, in contrast to speculative reason, pure practical reason does not stand in need of a critique, since its use is always within proper limits (CPrR, V: 15.1–16.12).[70] Nonetheless, pure practical reason is essential for rationalizing as the interest in being morally justified is an interest only of beings for whom violating duty can result in pangs of conscience and loss of self-esteem. Rationalizing would make no sense for an agent who does not acknowledge the authority of duty. Such an agent might still

---

[68] See Kant's discussion of the interests of (theoretical and practical) reason in the questions 'What can I know?', 'What should I do?', 'What may I hope?' (A/B: 804–5/832–3) and his discussion of the interest (practical and speculative) reason takes in the truth of the dogmatic theses of the antinomies (A/B: 462–76/490–504). Recently, Allais (2021) has proposed that, according to Kant, we have an interest in making 'sense of ourselves all the way down' (48), an interest which 'is a commitment that comes out of having practical reason' and 'explains our having an interest in self-deception' (48). This interest in self-understanding is different from the interest in being morally justified. I do not deny that agents tell themselves incorrect stories about their actions in order to maintain a narrative about themselves and that this is a very important phenomenon. However, I do think that, according to Kant, agents would be prone to rationalizing even if an immoral action did not threaten their self-conception, since these agents would still be subject to pangs of conscience and feelings of unworthiness and, independently of their self-conception, they have an interest in avoiding these pangs and feelings. Of course, agents might have an interest in self-understanding on top of the interest in moral justification, but I will focus on the latter, which pertains more immediately to the question of how agents deal with failure to live up to moral demands.

[69] In the Second Critique (CPrR, V: 119.27–120.10), Kant suggests that there is only a single interest of the pure practical use of reason, namely 'determination of the *will* with respect to the final and complete end'. I am not necessarily committed to the claim that the interest in moral justification is a *different* interest from the moral interest. The former could be the residual effects of the latter when an agent does not act out of respect.

[70] Kant later, however, acknowledges that '[p]ure reason always has its dialectic, whether it is considered in its speculative or in its practical use' (CPrR, V: 107.6–7).

deceive *others* to avoid punishment and criticism, but there would be no need for him to deceive *himself* about morality.

Moreover, there is textual evidence that Kant accorded pure practical reason a more ambivalent role than is often assumed. In a reflection from the mid- to late 1790s in which Kant discusses political revolution, he argues that moral agents demand that their 'innate rights' be respected by political authorities. They will even make use of violent and morally prohibited means, such as revolutions, to secure their rights against these authorities. Kant concedes that such a 'breach of law' is rooted in 'moral propensities', namely in an agent's awareness that they have inalienable rights. Being endowed with pure practical reason thus makes the agent prone to certain moral failings such as violent revolt in order to secure their rights (Ref, XIX: 611.12–25). We can find the same paradoxical structure in the *Metaphysics of Morals'* 'two crimes deserving death': a mother murdering her child because it is born out of wedlock and a soldier killing a fellow soldier in duel. It is the attempt to preserve one's *honour* that leads to both crimes, and honour 'is incumbent as a duty'.[71] Kant is aware that agents may act immorally because they seek to protect their special status as moral agents. They would not be incentivized to do so were it not for the authority they accord to morality and consequently to (their own) rights and honour.

The interest which incentivizes rationalizing is, so to speak, respect's *evil twin*, since both interests have their source in an agent's acknowledgement of the authority of morality, but one incentivizes us to do what is good while the other seeks excuses for what is bad if we failed to do the right thing, and even to justify it.[72] Paradoxically, the interest in being morally justified also makes rationalizing a negative vindication of the authority of morality. This vindication is *negative* since it manifests itself not in actions of moral worth, but in an offender's attempts to justify their behaviour to themselves. An offender seeking moral justification despite their transgressions demonstrates that morality still has a hold on them. Rationalizing *damages* an agent's conception of morality and commitment to duty, and at the same time *demonstrates* the never (completely) fading authority of morality.[73]

---

[71] MM, VI: 335.36–336.6; see also MM, VI: 420.26–30, 464.5–20; Eth-V, XXVII: 664.23–668.28. See also Moran's (2014: sec. 5) analysis of self-conceit in Kant as the tendency to convince oneself of one's virtue. This tendency can motivate genuinely moral actions as well as self-deception.

[72] Of course, if an agent acts from respect for the moral law they are justified in their action and hence satisfy the interest to be morally justified. Perhaps the cumbersome term 'interest in avoiding the bad effects of moral transgressions on one's happiness' is more fitting. However, as my discussion of the asymmetry of self-assessment below will show, the interest in being morally justified is present independently of prior moral transgressions and thus not just a matter of avoiding their negative consequences.

[73] See also Reath (2006: 20): 'Such behaviour reveals an underhand recognition of the authority of moral concerns. How else are we to understand these particular forms of dishonesty?'.

The pervasiveness of the interest in being morally justified is exhibited most clearly in Kant's doctrine of *Introspective Opacity*. Kant claims that we can never know that our actions are morally worthy. According to a standard reading of Kant, we have to know an action's motive in order to assess whether it was morally good, and we cannot know even our own motives with sufficient certainty to judge confidently that an action was motivated by duty.[74] To understand this claim correctly, it is important to note that Kant acknowledges that it is only morally *good* motives that are ultimately opaque,[75] and we can, in principle, know when an action *lacked* moral worth, for instance because it was not even in external accordance with duty.[76]

Kant worries that it is always possible that an action is motivated by an undetected, 'covert impulse of self-love' (G, IV: 407.9; see also G, IV: 419.25–31), but that the agent 'gladly flatters' themselves 'with the false presumption of a nobler motive' (G, IV: 407.11–12).[77] When an agent reaches the conclusion that they did something morally bad, they are warranted to believe that this is true, since they do not have an interest in thinking of themselves as morally bad (see Rel, VI: 37.18–23). If, however, they reach the conclusion that they acted from duty alone, they might always be deceiving themselves, since they do have an interest in being morally justified, and this interest biases self-assessment. Even an agent who always acted from duty cannot know for certain that they are morally good, since they can never fully trust their introspection. Kant thinks that an agent is not only interested in moral justification *after* the voice of conscience warns them not to commit an action, or after conscience reproaches them. The interest in being morally

---

[74] See Rel, VI: 38.7–12, 51.7–21, 70.1–71.20; MM, VI: 451.21–36. I cannot discuss here in any detail what Kant exactly maintains concerning the role of the right motivation, and whether the duty to act for the right motive applies to every single moral action or rather calls for a general and principled commitment to duty (see also my footnote 40). I take it that even on the latter reading Introspective Opacity persists and agents will want to know whether they are sufficiently committed to duty, but they can never be certain about this. I am grateful to Allen Wood for discussion of this issue.

[75] See A/B: 278/334, 551/579; G, IV: 451.21–36; Rel, VI: 25.5–6, 38.7–12, 51.7–21, 70.1–71.20, 70fn., 75.8–76.1; Sticker (2021b: 10).

[76] See G, IV: 407.1–16, 419.25–31; Rel, VI: 20.25–9; MM, VI: 392.30–393.3; TP, VIII: 284.21–285.11. See also Ware (2021: 136fn.5). Sometimes Kant even indicates that it is *easy* to identify bad motives; everything empirical that slips into the determination of the will '*makes itself known* at once' (CPrR, V: 92.3), and 'even children are capable of discovering the slightest taint of admixture of spurious incentives: for in their eyes the action then immediately loses all moral worth' (Rel, VI: 48.25–7). These claims must be overstatements, though. If all empirical incentives were easily detectable, we could infer that we acted from duty if we are unaware of any empirical incentives. Kant presumably means to say that brute inclinations can easily be cognized, but there are more subtle ways for empirical incentives to affect us.

[77] 'One is never more easily deceived than in what promotes a good opinion of oneself' (Rel, VI: 68.9–10).

justified is present independently of past moral violations, and it endangers all of our attempts of self-assessment.[78]

4.4 Common Human Reason

Sally Sedgwick (2008: 81) suggests that common human reason 'has the tendency to forget or even deceive itself about what it already knows'. Her view has textual support in G, IV: 405.30–1: '*in* practical common reason [. . .] a *dialectic* inadvertently unfolds' (first emphasis mine), that is, common human reason is the medium in which the dialectic unfolds. It has a tendency to 'forget' in the sense that agents endowed only with common human reason and without further instructions lack the means to effectively resist rationalizing (see also Section 3.1). However, I do not think that common human reason 'deceives itself about what it already knows', as Sedgwick suggests. After all, if common human reason was itself deceptive, then why would Kant aim to systematize and vindicate the common rational cognition of morality (see Section 2.3)?[79]

Without professional help common agents lack a systematic understanding of morality and of its underlying metaphysical assumptions and its source. They are thus unable to develop advanced strategies to defend their insights. Kant believes that the question as to what is the nature of the source of moral commands is, on the one hand, 'solely speculative' (RPT, VIII: 405.14–15). Lack of an answer does not change the fact that we have to obey moral commands. On the other hand, as long as it is not clear to agents that the source of morality is reason, they will represent the moral law as an '*oracle*' (RPT, VIII: 405.34).[80] The metaphor

---

[78] My proposed interest in being morally justified lends itself to recent *intellectualist* interpretations of Kant. Intellectualist interpreters believe that, according to Kant, 'all action carries an implicit claim to justification' (Reath 2006: 19), or that rational agents 'cannot adopt maxims without taking them to be, in some sense, justified (although this may very well rest on self-deception)' (Allison 1990: 91). The intellectualist framework 'assigns a significant role to rationalisation in Kant's conception of choice' (Reath 2006: 20). My conception is not straightforwardly intellectualist, though, since I acknowledge the existence of weakness of will and other cases of acting without deeming oneself justified (see Section 5.2). Intellectualists usually take issue with this phenomenon. However, see Morrisson (2005) for a proposal to reconcile weakness of will and central elements of intellectualism at least for non-moral actions. Moreover, Allison (1990: 158–61) understands weakness of will as a form of self-deception (see also my footnote 108).

[79] Most recently, common human reason was identified as a culprit for self-deception by Ware (2021: 20): 'we need a metaphysics of morals to protect common human reason from itself'. Of course, common human reason could be both a source of insight and responsible for self-deception, and, on balance, be worth preserving. I myself have argued that Kant is not unambiguously positive about common human reason (see Sticker 2017a). Yet, I do not think that any of the textual evidence for shortcomings of common human reason shows that common human reason is *deceptive* as opposed to merely being prone to being deceived.

[80] This warning occurs in Kant's 1796 essay on the *Noble* Tone, which is a critical reply to Romanticist appropriations of his philosophy. See also P, IV: 259.9–19; Anth, VII: 139.26–34 for similar warnings. Kant also warns of the 'prophetic spirit of sound reason' (P, IV: 314.8–9).

of the oracle reveals the problematic nature of common human reason. An oracle pronounces verdicts of great authority, but these verdicts often stand in need of 'interpretation' (RPT, VIII: 405.35). Frequently, their verdicts are ambiguous and can result in incorrect interpretations, though oracles do not straightforwardly lie.[81] Interpretations always run the danger of reading one's own preferred views into the object of interpretation. This is particularly dangerous when applied to morality, since an agent often has strong sensuous incentives to give moral commands a more lenient interpretation. If morality appears as an oracle, then there are plenty of occasions for misinterpretation and error.

In the *Religion*, Kant characterizes as 'inward deceit' a 'profession of reverence for the moral law which in its maxim does not however grant to the law preponderance over all other determining grounds'. Inward deceit is a 'lie to oneself in the interpretation of the moral law' (Rel, VI: 42fn.). It is the act of exploiting obscurities of one's conception of morality to interpret moral commands in a way that makes more room for inclination. Common human reason is not deceptive itself, but it is an *enabling condition* of self-deception as agents will sometimes believe that there is room for interpreting moral commands and even a need to do so. Moreover, a merely obscure grasp of morality makes it difficult to identify spurious interpretations. Hence, the natural dialectical tension unfolds *within* the obscure understanding of common human reason.

Explicit Categorical Imperative formulae can help agents understand that the moral law, when it issues perfect duties, is not an oracle that stands in need of interpretation. Perfect duties, according to Kant (MM, VI: 411.6–9), are always sufficiently clear and can be applied to specific cases without any quibbling about the role of inclinations. Furthermore, a systematic grasp of the system of duties and of how duties are grounded in different forms of contradiction (G, IV: 424) will help agents understand the differences between perfect and imperfect duties, and that only the latter, not the former, admit of latitude. The clearer it is to an agent what ought to be done in a situation, the easier it will be to resist seduction, since there is less room for ambiguities that can be exploited.

Pure practical reason, theoretical reason and common human reason are *enabling* conditions for self-deception, albeit in different ways. Without pure practical reason agents would see no point in engaging in rationalizing. By contrast, shortcomings of theoretical reason and common human reason make rationalizing easier. Speculation usually endangers the reasoning of the educated and philosophers, whereas the shortcomings of common human reason

---

[81] A classic example is the oracle received by Croesus as reported in Herodotus's *Histories* (1.53): 'if Croesus attacked the Persians, he would destroy a mighty empire'. Croesus interpreted this falsely as referring to the destruction of the *Persian* Empire. Herodotus also reports that oracles would blame humans for misunderstandings of their ambiguous verdicts (1.91).

affect everyone who lacks insight into the correct moral theory and source of morality.

4.5 Empirical Practical Reason

Empirical practical reason is more than just an enabling condition. It is the faculty to seek out and present supposed excuses and justifications. According to Henry Allison (2011: 143), empirical practical reason is of pivotal import-ance for the natural dialectic, as 'empirically conditioned practical reason creates the deceptive illusion of usurping the proper place of pure practical reason'.[82] Allison's focus on the role of empirical practical reason for rational-izing seemingly stands in tension with his focus on the role of *speculation* (see Section 4.2). We should keep in mind, though, that empirical practical reason can be interpreted as a part or aspect of theoretical reason, since it is concerned with '*technical*' advice concerning means-ends relations in the causal world of appearances.[83] Insofar as theoretical reason encompasses empirical practical reason it is indeed pivotal for rationalizing.

Empirical practical reason covers two different notions (G, IV: 415.6–418.1). First, imperatives of skill are imperatives to seek means to given ends. These ends might be obligatory, natural or personal. Second, empirical practical reason covers the capacity to harmonize one's inclinations 'into a whole called happiness' (Rel, VI: 58.5) and to promote specifically the ends conducive to one's personal happiness. Prudence is always 'in the service of the inclinations' (CPrR, V: 25.1; see also Rel, VI: 45.30–1), never in the service of obligatory ends, and it recommends external conformity to duty only as a means to avoid punishment, loss of self-esteem or pangs of conscience. This second aspect of empirical practical reason is central for rationalizing.

Inventing excuses and apparent justifications for immoral actions that further one's happiness is within the scope of prudence, since these excuses and apparent justifications can have three functions for an agent's happiness: (a) *Prospectively*, apparent justifications are sometimes necessary conditions for performing an action that one deems conducive to one's happiness but that one also takes to be immoral or at least open to moral criticism. Apparent justifica-tions can serve to convince oneself that a prudent action is morally permissible after all. (b) *Retrospectively*, apparent justifications or excuses may restore one's

---

[82] See also Henrich (1994: 66): 'Kant considers his entire philosophy an attempt to refute the sophistry of reason that is in the service of pleasure'.

[83] CPrR, V: 25.37–26.41; see also CPrR, V: 45.29–36; CJ, V: 172.14–22; FI, XX: 197.11–201.10. See Klingner (2012) and Kohl (2017b) for more. In addition, Allison specifically worries about *freedom* when he claims that only speculation endangers common human reason (see Allison 2011: 350). Freedom has both theoretical and practical dimensions.

self-esteem when they serve to convince oneself that a supposedly immoral action was excusable or even justified. (c) *Prospectively* and *retrospectively*, deeming oneself morally justified will make one feel deserving of the happiness one has obtained or is striving for.

On my interpretation, prudence is not merely concerned with discovering external means that would further happiness, but also with *internal means*, such as excuses and justifications. Kant himself stresses that we have a 'legal adviser (defence counsel)' before the internal court of conscience.[84] Since the verdicts of the court of reason affect an agent's happiness, it is plausible to assume that prudence is this advocate. Prudence is not only 'a servant of natural inclination' (Rel, VI: 45.30–1), but it is also its advocate. In the *Kaehler Lecture Notes*, the internal advocate is called a 'twister of the law' [*Rechtsverdreher*] (Eth-K, 201; see also Eth-C, XXVII: 359.14). This derogatory term is a fitting metaphor. *Rechtsverdreher* are lawyers who stick to the letter of the law but who make use of loopholes and ambiguities in order to further the interests of their clients. They thus 'make use of the letter of the law' to undermine its spirit (Eth-K: 201). This approach, according to Kant, is 'sin' when applied to the moral law (Rel, VI: 30.29–34).[85]

The deceptive aspect of our rationality comes closest to what Kant sometimes refers to as *homo phaenomenon*: a finite rational agent whose reason is in the service of inclinations (see MM, VI: 439.30–1). We can see now that Kant gets it almost completely the wrong way around when he suggests in MM, VI: 430.13–16 that the internal lie could be performed by the *homo noumenon* who uses the 'natural being (*homo phaenomenon*) as a mere means'. The *homo noumenon* or pure practical reason is a necessary condition for rationalizing, but the activity of rationalizing itself, if any rational sub-faculty can be said to be active in this process, is one of empirical practical reason or of the *homo phaenomenon*. Prudence makes use of the rich material provided by an agent's social surroundings and religious doctrine, metaphysical speculations as well as

---

[84] MM, VI: 439fn.35; see also MM, VI: 440.20–4; Eth-P, XXVII: 197.30–2; Eth-V, XXVII: 618.23–4; Eth-K: 193, 200. In the *Collins* lecture notes from the 1770s, Kant specifies that our 'advocate' before the internal court is 'self-love', which 'excuses [the agent] and makes many an objection to the accusation' (Eth-C, XXVII: 354.20–1; see also Moeller 2020: ch. 6). Of course, self-love as such cannot advance excuses or apparent justifications, since this requires rational capacities. Self-love is merely the reason why agents rather listen to excuses and apparent justification than to their conscience.

[85] In Sticker (2016a: 100), I propose that we understand empirical practical reason as a *sophist* rather than a lawyer. The metaphor of a lawyer defending a client was taken up without reference to Kant by Haidt (2001) to describe the process of motivated reasoning. Kant would readily agree with Haidt that one function of reason is that of an internal lawyer. However, reason can also be an impartial judge. Haidt presumably would not deny this, but he thinks that the impartiality of reason and reasoning's power to overturn one's judgements has been overemphasized by philosophers.

of the shortcomings of common human reason in order to promote an agent's sensuous ends at the expense of morality. Rationalizing is thus truly an 'abuse' (UPT, VIII: 161.27) of rational capacities and a turning of reason against itself.[86]

5 Apparent Justifications, Ideology and Uncritical Philosophy

We now understand how rationalizing is a use and an abuse of reason. Two important issues still remain, though. First, we saw that rationalizing would be pointless for an agent who completely renounced morality. How can agents engage in rationalizing without losing their grasp of the moral law entirely and without ceasing to be morally responsible and concerned about moral justification? Second, how can a rationalizer ever hope to successfully think of a moral violation as justified? No matter how subtle the rationalizing, a morally forbidden action can never come out as truly justified. But if rationalizing would always be in vain, then why would agents be in constant danger of engaging in it? We rather would expect that agents, at some point, realize that rationalizing is pointless and that, from then on, they reason according to the full strictness and purity of the moral law and suffer deserved pangs of conscience for their transgressions. This, however, would be in tension with Kant's belief that the danger of succumbing to rationalizing always remains.[87]

Kant clearly thinks that rationalizing is not completely futile. Conscience can be 'stunned' and 'put to sleep' temporarily (MM, VI: 438.13–23), and we can administer 'opium', a sedative, to it (Rel, VI: 78.32–5) and provide it with 'a cushion' on which it is meant to 'sleep quietly' (Ped, IX: 495.13–15).[88] However, even the most thorough self-deceiver cannot avoid 'waking up from time to time' and hearing the voice of conscience (MM, VI: 438.13–23). Kant also states that a wrongdoer can 'consider himself to be justified before the law', and that there can be undeserved 'peace of conscience' [*Gewissensruhe*] (Rel, VI: 38.11–23). These passages also show that rationalizers do not merely seek

---

[86] See also Sherman (1997: 134): 'Rationalization is reason's own corruption of itself'.

[87] There is a related problem for Kant's conception of rationalizing: how is it possible to falsely deem oneself justified or excused, given that agents are endowed with an infallible mechanism of self-assessment: *conscience*? According to Kant, 'an *erring* conscience is an absurdity' (MM, VI: 401.3–5; see also MM, VI: 401.8; MPT, VIII: 268.10–13; Eth-V, XXVII: 615.32–6; Eth-K: 195). Humans may 'artificialize' [*künsteln*] as much as they want to represent moral transgressions as an 'unintentional fault' or mere 'oversight' but their 'advocate' before conscience cannot 'reduce to silence the prosecutor within' (CPrR, V: 98.13–21; see also Rel, VI: 77.27). I discuss agents' attempts to avoid conscience's reprimands in Sticker (2016a),where I argue that Kant's model of an internal court is inadequate to account for the pervasive threat self-deception poses. In addition, I am sceptical of Kant's claims that conscience is infallible (Sticker 2020a).

[88] See also Eth-K: 135; Eth-C, XXVII: 357.4–5.

to excuse themselves. They ultimately aim for full justification, and this can be seemingly achieved at least temporarily.[89]

I will now argue that we should understand corruption as adopting a form of ideology that superimposes itself onto one's original grasp of morality. Corrupted agents deem themselves justified in their moral violations, but they are still able to see through their spurious reasoning and thus do not escape moral commands and responsibility (Section 5.1). I will then sketch the development from innocence to full-fledged corruption and misleading ethical theory (Section 5.2). This will establish that Kant acknowledges that rationalizers can be in a state of false (though not complete) certainty, and it will illustrate in what sense rationalizing can achieve its goal.

5.1 Apparent Justifications and Ideology

Moral transgressions, for Kant, can never be justified. In this sense, all rationalizing is in vain. Agents can, however, find 'subjective reasons' (Eth-V, XXVII: 617.2–3) and 'subjective grounds of consolation' (Eth-V, XXVII: 618.38–619.1) for moral violations. These reasons are 'subjective' because they cannot withstand thorough scrutiny by other agents or the agent themselves if they think about them in an unbiased manner.

Apparent justifications (as well as excuses) are psychological means to cope with one's failure to live up to the demands of the moral law. They share important structural properties with genuine justifications; they are meant to apply to *all* agents in relevantly similar circumstances, and they cover a *multitude* of similar cases. When we (actually, or merely apparently) justify an action, we believe that others, if they are unbiased, would accept this justification, and others can, in principle, appeal to this justification as well. Furthermore, we believe that what justifies our actions in one situation will also justify (or at least count in favour of) similar actions in relevantly similar situations. Deeming oneself justified implies to 'at least implicitly [. . .] believe that there is some sort of general point to what one is doing' (Ameriks 2012: 158).[90] Apparent justifications therefore do not merely seemingly sanction one-off transgressions, but potentially condone systematic violations of the moral law.

This element of systematicity is succinctly captured by Andrews Reath (2006: 20) when he states that, in the act of rationalizing, the agent adopts an

---

[89] Kant also stresses that the cult aims to 'justify before God', not merely to excuse transgressions (Rel, VI: 174.27–30). Moreover, see Rel, VI: 38.12–17, 174.27–30; MPT, VIII: 268.26–269.1; Eth-V, XXVII: 619.36–620.8 for examples of agents who falsely believe themselves to be morally justified.

[90] This is a version of the more general point that it is in the nature of reasons to be universal, a central element of a number of Kantian approaches (e.g., Korsgaard 2009: 72–3).

'ideology [. . .] which enables individuals to view their maxims as objectively acceptable reasons'. An *ideology* is not simply a set of false beliefs but a system of beliefs devised to promote an agenda, in this case the agenda of one's sensuous nature.[91] An ideology has to be *systematic* at least in the sense of being internally consistent and comprised of propositions that support each other to some extent.[92] After all, a mere collection of unrelated claims (let alone contradictory ones) could hardly confer an apparent justification. It is more difficult to correct an agent who has adopted an ideology than to correct someone who merely holds an aggregate of discreet incorrect beliefs (see Eth-K: 157–8). The former has constructed a pseudo-rational protection against rational criticism. This is especially so if the ideology provides explanations for why others would object to it ('Of course, the Man would want me to believe this. . .'). The rationalizer thus can avail themselves of replies to potential criticism.

Importantly, Kant believes that ideologies cannot be all-encompassing. Completely denying the validity of the moral law 'before one's reason [. . .] is impossible for a human being' (MM, VI: 321.40–322.20), and even the worst human being 'does not repudiate the moral law, whatever [their] maxims, in rebellious attitude (by revoking obedience to it)' (Rel, VI: 36.1–7).[93] Even the most hardened scoundrel in *Groundwork* III still at least 'wishes' to have the right disposition, and acknowledges the higher status of their rational self (G, IV: 454.20–455.9). However, while rational agents always acknowledge the importance of being moral, they might develop conceptions of morality that seemingly make it easier to be moral than a strict and pure moral law does.

As I explained (Section 2.2), both Papish and Grenberg assume that rational-izers acknowledge the need for help and that rationalizers can never be certain in their incorrect views. I sympathize with this view insofar as it emphasizes that rationalizing can never lead to absolute certainty and can never completely eclipse one's original conception of morality (see below in this section). However, I also think that this assumption underestimates the danger of

---

[91] The connection between rationalizing and ideology is also stressed by Piper (2008: 364) and Allais (2021). See also Railton (1986: 202–3): 'La Rochefoucauld wrote that hypocrisy is the tribute vice pays to virtue, but "hypocrisy" suggests cynicism. We might better say that ideology is the respect partisans show to impartiality'. Wehofsits (2020: 22) proposes the term 'delusion' specifically for those cases in which the rationalization of a *passion* 'distorts the agent's view of reality to such an extent that she is hardly able to correct the distortion anymore'.

[92] Kant's own notion of a system is much more demanding than this; a system is 'the unity of the manifold cognitions under one idea'. This idea 'is the rational concept of the form of a whole, insofar as through this the domain of the manifold as well as the position of the parts with respect to each other is determined a priori' (A/B: 832/860).

[93] See also CPrR, V: 152.9–18; Rel, VI: 46.1–5, 77.26–7; MM, VI: 321.40–322.20, 464.1–3; Anth, VII: 293.28–294.2; Eth-V, XXVII: 574.35–575.1; Eth-K: 99.

rationalizing. The reason for this underestimation might be rooted in an ambiguity in the term 'certainty'. There is a sense in which a rationalizer can never be certain and one in which they can be. Certainty can be rationally warranted, namely if it is certainty in the truth of a well-justified proposition that can withstand rational scrutiny. A rationalizer indeed cannot have this type of certainty, since rationalizing cannot produce justifications that survive unbiased scrutiny. Certainty can also be merely subjective, namely the kind of unwarranted certainty that a fallible and imperfect agent might have in a belief even though this belief is, in fact, unjustified. Certainty of the latter kind can be the result of rationalizing or of other mistakes in reasoning, and such a certainty can be psychologically powerful, action-guiding and difficult to overcome.

I should note that one reason why I emphasize that Kant acknowledges that agents can be subjectively certain of their mistaken views is that I regard this as a charitable interpretation. My interpretation allows Kant to account for important and widespread phenomena; rationalizers often do not give up their views easily, they assert them with great confidence, they try to convince others (and might succeed in doing so) and they even form group identities around their rationalizations.[94]

This interpretation, however, raises the question of whether a rationalizer who is certain and steadfast in their false convictions can still be subject to deserved criticism. Importantly, there are degrees of certainty and Kant maintains that rationalizers are never *completely* certain, not even subjectively so. Rationalizers, even in a state of false certainty, are still agents who have not entirely lost their connection to the moral law. Such agents *can* still judge correctly, but it is much more difficult for them, as there are additional epistemic hurdles that they themselves have put in their way.

Unfortunately, Kant provides few detailed descriptions of the reasoning of thoroughly self-deceived agents. To understand how even very corrupted agents can never be *absolutely* certain, let us look at the two cases that most clearly exhibit corruption at work.

---

[94] Papish (2018: 109) herself provides a very instructive example for this: 'Much like how racial ideologies undergo a metamorphosis in which beliefs that initially promoted material pleasure can outstrip their initial purposes, so too can we develop passions whose connection to our more basic material interests becomes increasingly attenuated.' Papish thinks self-deception should primarily be understood as a violation of epistemic norms, such as not paying attention to evidence. However, her example, a racist ideology that is initially supposed to justify economic exploitation but that persists even once the economic realities have changed, is not one of rationalizers merely shifting focus or distracting themselves from the truth. Rather, the ideologues here are presumably convinced of their own superiority over others. To understand the danger of rationalizing, we must bear in mind that violations of epistemic norms can lead to practical misconceptions that agents feel certain of.

First, we already saw (Section 3.2) that the kind of reasoning that can lead agents to eudaemonism is a paradigm of rationalizing. It is instructive how Kant describes one of the chief advocates of eudaemonism of his time, *Christian Garve*. Garve denies that duty can be independent of the prospect of personal happiness (TP, VIII: 284.9–285.22).[95] He does not hear the voice of reason as a voice of pure practical reason, but as a recommendation for how to attain happiness. According to Kant, this mistake is primarily a *theoretical* one. The moral law still speaks to Garve and he can find in his '*heart*' (TP, VIII: 285.13) the motivation to follow its commands. The mistake is in Garve's 'head' (TP, VIII: 285.15), or one of 'speculation' (TP, VIII: 285.18). Garve cannot conceive of a motive for actions other than personal happiness and thus he falsely assumes that this must also be the motive for moral actions. He has adopted the wrong metaphysical framework to understand the possibility of acting from duty. This does not mean that he denies the authority of duty, but merely that his philosophy is incapable of accounting for this authority.[96] While Garve stands in need of correction, Kant maintains that his eudaemonist ideology does not strip him of moral agency.

Garve, like other academically educated and sophisticated people, has bought into theoretical misconceptions (see Section 4.2). However, Kant maintains that Garve has not completely given up on the commitments he holds qua being rational. Kant presumably assumes that if confronted with scenarios such as the Gallows Case (see Section 2.3), Garve can be brought to admit that he could do what he acknowledges he ought to do, even though he might initially be certain that sacrificing one's life merely for the sake of duty is impossible. Garve still has in his 'heart' the right insights, and if we put him in a situation that allows him to abstract from his theoretical misconceptions, we can elicit moral responses from him that he cannot account for in his own theory and that prove his eudaemonist framework wrong.[97]

Second, we also saw (Section 3.2) that the religious cult is a source of ideology *par excellence*. It creates supposed grounds of excuses, apparent

---

[95] Kant here refers to Garve's criticism of the Second Critique. See Henrich (1967: 133–52) for the relevant sections from Garve.

[96] Kant maintains a similar line in his discussions of other philosophers. Spinoza denies the existence of God and immortality of the soul. However, he is a 'righteous man' (CJ, V: 452.8–453.5; see also Eth-K: 125–6; A/B: 745–6/773–4) for whom it is difficult to explain why actions from duty are not futile. Epicurus is virtuous since his hedonism is only supposed to *explain* actions but not intended as a theory of the proper moral *motivation* (CPrR, V: 115.25–116.20; see also MM, VI: 485.5; Eth-C, XXVII: 395.20–5). Epicurus is, like Garve, an agent whose philosophy has affected his *explanation* of moral actions, but for whom actions from duty are still possible. He is confused, but only partly deaf (see Section 5.2).

[97] Of course, it remains an assumption on Kant's part that the Gallows Case is so clear that even a eudaemonist would concede that they can and should sacrifice their life in this situation. See Sticker (2020b: sec. 5) for discussion.

justifications and means to seemingly escape one's responsibility. In the *Religion*, Kant describes an extreme case of an agent influenced by such an ideology: an 'inquisitor' [*Ketzerrichter*] (Rel, VI: 186.21) who is 'firm in the belief' (Rel, VI: 186.30) that he ought 'to take a human being's life because of his religious faith' (Rel, VI: 186.36–7). However, even this inquisitor 'could not have been entirely certain' (Rel, VI: 186.29) that putting to death the heretic is right. According to Kant, the inquisitor can still be criticized for violating the principle 'that we *ought to venture nothing where there is a danger that it might be wrong*' (Rel, VI: 186.23–4). This safety principle would not apply if the inquisitor were absolutely certain and unaware of the moral danger of his course of action.[98] After all, the principle is best understood as requiring that we refrain from doing something if we are *aware* of even a small danger that it is wrong, since it is difficult to see how agents could be required to be cautious without any awareness on their part of potential wrongness. Thus, Kant maintains that even in extreme cases of being in the grip of a murderous ideology an agent can never be absolutely certain. The inquisitor is in principle still able to see through the ideology he adopted and thus does not escape all responsibility.[99]

Both cases demonstrate that Kant thinks that while rationalizing can lead to false beliefs about duty and even to ideologies that agents advocate publicly and that they defend against objections and act on with great conviction, rationalizing cannot be *all-encompassing* in the sense that the moral law is completely replaced and it becomes impossible for an agent to act from duty. Rationalizing can only lead to *modifications* of one's initial conception of morality. An ideology is not adopted *instead* of the moral law, but as an *addition*. An agent in the grip of an ideology will still treat the moral law as a point of reference, but they will also treat factors other than universality and humanity as relevant for their deliberation. As a result of this, an agent's moral deliberation becomes more *complex* than the supposedly easy and straightforward universality- and humanity-based reflections outlined in Section 2.3. For Kant, as we will see in the next section, there is something deficient about an agent who stands in need

---

[98] I am grateful to Jens Timmermann for many discussions of the inquisitor case. He ultimately convinced me that the inquisitor is not absolutely certain (not even subjectively so). See Timmermann (2020: 224).

[99] Hill and Boxill (2001: 470) argue that Kant was mistaken 'to suppose we can always overcome our self-deception, and bring the morally relevant facts vividly before us, by a sufficiently strenuous rational self-examination'. It is true that Kant is very optimistic about the power of the voice of reason to cut through self-deception. However, he does acknowledge that there could be extreme cases. When Kant claims that conscience cannot be bribed, he warns that this only holds for those 'not of the worst sort' (Rel, VI: 77.21). Likewise, he qualifies that the most hardened scoundrel acknowledges the authority of morality 'if only he is otherwise in the habit of using reason' (G, IV: 454.22).

of too much reflection about a moral case – one might call this the Kantian version of Bernard Williams's famous *One Thought Too Many* problem.

5.2 The Story of Corruption

We can now tell the full story of the corruption of common agents. As a finite being with needs and inclinations an agent will not always comply with the commands of duty, even if these commands are clear to them and they are aware of the commands' authority. Kant acknowledges that agents can act without taking themselves to be morally justified at the time of acting. He calls this phenomenon 'frailty *(fragilitas)*' (Rel, VI: 29.24–30), the first of three grades of evil in the *Religion*;[100] an agent is aware of what they ought to do and has 'incorporated the good (the law)' (Rel, VI: 29.26) into their maxim but their motivation to act on this maxim is too weak. This phenomenon is more commonly referred to as *weakness of will*.[101]

Besides frailty, Kant acknowledges two slightly different ways in which agents do something without deeming themselves justified. An agent can be overwhelmed by an *affect*, a precipitate or rash feeling, and fail to think about justification at all. Affects lead to temporary loss of one's rational capacities and can 'at once' make rational deliberation impossible.[102] In addition, *passions* can 'remove' one's 'freedom of mind'.[103] They are lasting and habitual sensuous inclinations, and they remove an agent's capacity for self-determination because an agent, when in the grip of a passion, considers situations only as opportunities for or hindrances to the satisfaction of their passion. Affects even undermine means-ends reasoning (Anth, VII: 253.31–3), whereas passions can be in place together with instrumental uses of reason to determine the best means to satisfy the passion.[104]

In both of these cases, the agent did not consider the morality of what they are doing.[105] These failings are different from frailty. They rather constitute

---

[100] I cannot undertake a discussion of *radical evil* here. Allison (2011: 143) claims that there is a 'virtual equivalence' between the natural dialectic and propensity to evil. I believe that the doctrine of radical evil goes beyond Kant's *Groundwork* conception in that it holds that we must regard our ineradicable propensity to violate the moral law as natural *and* self-chosen (Rel, VI: 32.13–33), whereas the natural dialectical tension results from our double natures and is not due to choice.

[101] See also A/B: 808/836; G, IV: 406.8–25, 413.12–18; Rel, VI: 37.18–26; MM, VI: 379.15–380.6; Anth, VII: 293.28–294.2; Eth-K: 204–5 for Kant's discussions of this phenomenon.

[102] Anth, VII: 267.8; see also Anth, VII: 251.15–19, 252.3–6; MM, VI: 407.21–408.2.

[103] CJ, V: 272.30–7; see also Rel, VI: 29.36–7; Anth, VII: 267.9; Ref, XV: 459.8

[104] See MM, VI: 407.29–408.14; Anth, VII: 252.20–1, 265.34–5. Passions are not only a danger for morality but also '*pragmatically* ruinous' (Anth, VII: 267.6), because the satisfaction of all of one's other inclinations is put on hold.

[105] It is important to note that passions 'come in various degrees' and 'not all passions are all-encompassing' (Formosa 2009: 204). Moreover, since passions can be long-lasting, agents can

a failure to act in the strict Kantian sense (in the case of affects)[106] or to morally reflect about one's actions (in the case of passions). Still, in all three cases agents lack a proper justification, because they either act against what they are aware they ought to do, or what they do lacks any concern for (moral) justification. Agents are either aware of their lack of justification at the time of acting (frailty) or can become aware of it retrospectively (affects and passions).

Frailty, affects and passions alone cannot corrupt, since they leave one's conception of morality untouched.[107] Nonetheless, they can give rise to the attempt to retrospectively find excuses for one's unjustified behaviour. If upon critical reflection an agent realizes that their action was morally unjustified – and presumably even more so if they were aware of this during their action – they will experience pangs of conscience and loss of self-esteem. The agent will be tempted to 'hide' from 'the voice [of reason] which makes even the boldest evildoer tremble' (CPrR, V: 80.1–2). They will enter a process of ex post rationalizing. Rationalizing thus usually begins with calling the strictness of morality into question to retrospectively find excuses.[108]

---

critically reflect on them when in a (relatively) calm state. This reflection can, however, be biased and a form of rationalizing that might even reinforce the passion. Moreover, I take it that at least in the case of strong passions there is no critical reflection immediately prior to action, but at most instrumental calculation. See Wehofsits (2016) for more detailed discussion of affects and passions. Wehofsits (2020: 3) even proposes, largely based on textual evidence from the *Anthropology*, that rationalizing 'primarily aims at resolving a psychological conflict between passion and moral duty'. I do agree with her that passions are significant for rationalizing, but Kant's most prominent discussions of rationalizing and examples thereof in works other than the *Anthropology* by no means restrict rationalizing to a conflict between duty and *passions*. Rather, the conflict is between duty and inclinations more generally. I am grateful to Anna Wehofsits and Laura Papish for discussion of the role of passions in Kant.

[106] I agree with Frierson (2014: 215) that being overwhelmed by affects is different from frailty, since frailty is a form of evil and the ground of evil must lie in a maxim (Rel, VI: 21.9–12), whereas being overwhelmed by affects does not constitute acting on a maxim but rather failure to act. See also Vujosevic (2018: 44–6) for discussion.

[107] Hill (2012: 144) correctly points out that weak-willed persons do have a commitment 'to follow the full, unqualified prescriptions of their rational legislative will' but fail to live up to this commitment on particular occasions. The merely weak-willed person's conception of morality is still without 'loopholes' (2012: 120). Papish (2018: 60), by contrast, argues that there cannot be a strict distinction between frailty and impurity, the second grade of evil, as frailty is often used as a pretext by an agent with impure maxims. I agree that frailty can be a pretext, but this does not mean that frailty cannot be distinguished from impurity (see also Rukgaber 2015). I should also note that passions might be able to corrupt agents, since they can become bound up with one's identity, and gain a stronger hold due to rationalizing (see my footnote 105). This can impact an agent's understanding of morality. However, I take it that this is the result of having passions over a prolonged period of time, not of individual actions committed from passions.

[108] I do not think that it is *always* or *necessarily* the case that rationalizing begins this way. This is only typically so. Kant indicates in two passages that *inward-deceit*, a form of self-deception, and not frailty, is 'the main ground of evil' in human beings (Rel, VI: 42fn.; see also MM, VI: 431.5–15 and Section 4.4). This would suggest that self-deception precedes frailty. Kant, however, admits that he here turns 'what must be thought objectively first by nature' into what 'appears first in time' (Rel, VI: 41.33–5). His claims are not intended as a thesis about the

At this point, an agent's commitment to morality has already become conditional in an important sense; the agent thinks that certain external factors or grounds of excuses can mitigate moral violations. However, empirical factors are not yet part of the agent's conception of what morality commands. Nonetheless, excuses can become more numerous and more elaborate and, at some point, the agent will deem certain transgressions not only excusable but will stop seeing them as transgressions. They believe that what excused their behaviour in retrospection also must have an impact on the question of whether they are under a particular obligation at all. After all, if they truly believe to have found a sound excuse, then they will at least suspect that they have uncovered a morally salient factor, such as that there are certain sacrifices morality cannot reasonably expect of them or that violating supposed moral rules is permissible if the overall outcome is a good one, and that these factors also should inform their ex ante deliberations. Anything that truly excuses actions in retrospection also seems to matter for moral deliberation. Kant acknowledges that there can be genuine excuses that mitigate responsibility (see MM, VI: 228.11–22). However, he is also concerned that agents are overly lenient with themselves and search for (and seemingly find) excuses instead of earnestly trying to improve themselves, and, even worse, that agents come to believe that supposed excuses can *justify* their actions.

An agent who has made excuses part of their very conception of what morality commands is *confused*. They still apply common universalization tests in their reasoning, and they are aware that certain ways of treating other rational agents are simply wrong, but they also have adopted convictions that can interfere with their moral reasoning. A system of pseudo-justifications has superimposed itself onto the rationalizer's original grasp of morality. As

---

genesis of evil but about the most important mechanism of corruption. According to an influential reading of the degrees of evil by Allison (1990: 158–60), 'self-deception enters the picture at the very beginning' (159). However, I think that the admittedly central role of self-deception for Kant does not imply that evil and corruption must start with rationalizing. It is (textually and otherwise) more plausible to assume that rationalizing normally enters the picture once an agent tries to come to terms with previous immoral behaviour. There is something artificial about constructing all cases of wrongdoing as products of self-deception. This is especially so since being overcome by affects, and maybe also by passions, does not constitute an action in the full sense of the term. These phenomena are not necessarily expressive of an agent's freedom and not something they are fully responsible for. Maintaining that agents are responsible even for morally bad actions is, however, the chief underlying motive for Allison's claim that self-deception is operational all the way down. See also Rukgaber (2015: 235), who argues that frailty is a form of 'clear-eyed weakness of will (strict *akratic* action)' and a 'form of practical irrationality without self-deception'. Most recently, Welsch (2019) has stressed correctly that while self-deception and radical evil together constitute an evil disposition, these components are distinct, and that self-deception is not the ground of all evil. Formosa (2009: 199) likewise stresses that, for Kant, self-deception is not a necessary feature of all deliberate evildoing.

I explained (Section 3.3), an agent who has allowed morally irrelevant considerations to enter their moral deliberation, even when they act from what they think is duty, is likely to act from the additional concerns that they deem significant. Performing the right external actions, but not from duty, is what Kant labels 'impurity' [*Unlauterkeit*], the second grade of evil.

I should note that the relation between rationalizing against purity in *Groundwork* 405 and impurity as a grade of evil is not straightforward, since Kant uses two different German terms: *Reinheit* [*Groundwork*] and *Unlauterkeit* [*Religion*], commonly translated as 'purity' and 'impurity' respectively. However, the latter is not simply the negation of the former. *Reinheit* is broader, as it concerns motivational and cognitive aspects of morality (see Section 3.2), whereas *Unlauterkeit* is merely a question of motivation. In fact, as we saw (see Section 3.2), the cognitive component of *Reinheit* precedes the motivational one. The *Religion*'s *Unlauterkeit* and the *Groundwork*'s motivational component of impurity presuppose that agents make empirical concerns part of their conception of morality.[109]

The rationalizer has devised a system of caveats, qualifications and provisos that condition their commitment to the moral law. They will ultimately only obey the moral law if no other considerations, such as supposedly good consequences, their own projects that come with a supposed moral status and son on, present themselves as more salient than universalizability and humanity. Such a conditional commitment to the moral law can even result in plainly wrong judgements about duty and in believing themselves justified when committing externally wrong actions. Moreover, a conditional commitment to morality like this is called 'wickedness' or '*perversity*' in the *Religion*, the third grade of evil (Rel, VI: 30.9–18), and 'corruption' in the *Groundwork*. Importantly, in the *Groundwork*, Kant introduces corruption not as an attribute of an *agent*, but of the *strictness of the moral law* (G, IV: 405.15–17).[110] Since the moral law *itself* cannot be corrupted, corruption must pertain to an agent's *conception* of the moral law, or, more precisely, to their conception of 'strict laws of duty' (G, IV: 405.14). The immediate target of rationalizing is not the moral law as such, but *laws* (note the plural 'strenge Gesetze der Pflicht') of duty, or specific duties in specific situations. A rationalizer is still committed to morality as such, but does

---

[109] Rukgaber (2015: 254–5) argues that the second grade of evil, *Unlauterkeit*, also encompasses cognitive mistakes, since sometimes questions of motivation and intention are relevant for judging whether an action is permissible. If this is correct, then *Unreinheit* and *Unlauterkeit* might be similar after all.

[110] See also: 'No greater crime can be found than *seeking to corrupt the moral law*, and thus there is nothing more harmful than a lax ethics, namely when the law accommodates itself to evil opinion. The ethical law is a punctual and strict law that requires perfection in the highest degree' (Eth-P, XXVII: 164.5–10; my emphasis).

not want to accept the burdensome commands that follow from a strict and pure moral law. However, when they rationalize against some of their specific duties, they end up modifying their conception of morality, since they make assumptions that are incompatible with the strictness and purity of morality. This, Kant believes, 'reverses the ethical order' (Rel, VI: 30.13–14), an order that requires unconditional obedience to duty in all its strictness and purity.

Even though rationalizing primarily serves the purpose of making more room for an agent's *own* inclinations and personal projects, it also jeopardizes the capacity to judge about cases not immediately involving oneself. This is important because it allows Kant to explain how agents can be mistaken even in evaluations of hypothetical scenarios with no prospect of loss or reward to themselves. The ideology that results from rationalizing 'puts out of tune the moral ability to judge what to think of a human being' (Rel, VI: 38.28–9). The metaphor 'out of tune' [*verstimmt*] is fitting, since an instrument that is out of tune *consistently* plays false notes, just as a corrupted agent's judgements might consistently follow a false pattern. An ideology impacts the way an agent judges their own actions as well as the actions of *other* agents and of *hypothetical* cases, since it contains general claims about what is morally justifiable. In fact, an ideology is more convincing the more it appears to be based on unprejudiced, disinterested factors that seemingly pertain to all cases and all agents alike.

Kant warns that 'dishonesty, by which we throw dust in our own eyes [...] extends itself also externally, to falsity or deception of others' (Rel, VI: 38.23–6). The sheer quantity of others' immoral activities already suggests an excuse for not being moral; others are manifestly immoral, so why should I be (much) better?[111] In addition, agents demand justifications or excuses from each other for harmful or disrespectful actions. A self-deceived offender is likely to think that they have nothing to hide, and that a convincing justification for *them* will also be one for *others*, and they will present their apparent justifications to them. If an interlocutor buys into the rationalizer's story, they might consider themselves justified in similar cases. By entering the practice of demanding and providing (pseudo-)justifications as well as (pseudo-)excuses, agents throw dust into each other's eyes. This practice can inspire new strategies for rationalizing and agents can reinforce each other in this. A particular danger of the social sphere is that some agents are figures of (social and religious) authority and seemingly in a position to propose and validate justifications and excuses (see Section 3.2).[112]

---

[111] 'It suffices that they are there, that they surround him, and that they are human beings, and they will mutually corrupt each other's moral disposition' (Rel, VI: 94.4–6). See also Wood (1999: 283–91).

[112] It is well established that the social sphere, with its hierarchies and group loyalties, is a rich source of self-deception. See for instance Anderson (2016: 93), who stresses that '[p]ower

As the structure of the *Groundwork* reveals, rationalizing is, according to Kant, closely connected to one particular form of public ideology: *popular philosophy*. Following his discussion of the natural dialectical tension, at the beginning of *Groundwork* II Kant criticizes popular philosophy as an inadequate response to the natural dialectic. Popular philosophers promise help to those who have become confused about duty. However, they present a 'disgusting mish-mash of gleaned observations and half-rationalizing principles' (G, IV: 409.30–2; see also G, IV: 426.18–19; JL, IX: 148.11–18). They combine various elements from virtue ethics, theology, moral-sense theory, perfectionism and so on, but they do so without providing a unifying rational principle (G, IV: 410.3–18).[113] Even worse, their teachings amplify confusion because they make an agent 'waver' (G, IV: 411.7) in their reasoning between the various elements that they present. Kant is concerned that popular philosophy, as a form of collective rationalizing, reinforces rationalizing and inspires new strategies thereof, rather than helping agents to overcome it.

Kant is aware that philosophers have the training and skills to earnestly inquire into the foundations of morality, but the same training and skills can be used to please the taste of the public and to seemingly justify moral transgressions.[114] In the Second Critique, Kant claims that common agents hear the voice of reason clearly, and only the 'head-confusing [*kopfverwirrende*] speculations of the schools [. . .] are brazen enough to make oneself deaf to that heavenly voice' (CPrR, V: 35.16–18; my trans.),[115] and that 'only

---

makes people morally blind. It stunts their moral imaginations and corrupts their moral reasoning, tripping them up in contradictions and sophistries.' Shared ideologies also frequently serve as justifications for violence against or exploitation of members of outgroups (cf. Graham 2020), and can conceal our own involvement in unjust structures (see Allais 2021). Kant even thinks that it is already a problem if agents compare themselves with others (as opposed to with the inflexible standard of the moral law), regardless of social biases and ideologies that might skew this comparison even more (MM, VI: 435.31–7; Eth-K: 313–14). It should be noted that the scepticism towards the social world Kant here expresses is not shared by many contemporary theorists of rationalizing, such as Haidt (2001), Schwitzgebel and Ellis (2017) and Mercier and Sperber (2018), who emphasize that collaborative thinking frequently produces better results and is less biased than solitary reasoning.

[113] Moreover, these elements are all impure (see Sticker 2017a: sec. 3).

[114] Kant sometimes even uses 'philosophizing' [*philosophieren*] in the sense of 'rationalizing'; agents can 'philosophize themselves out of' a commitment and thus damage the steadfastness of their character (L-F, XXV: 624.7–16). In a Kantian spirit, Piper (2008: 296) points out that we, philosophers, are ideally equipped to rationalize, due to 'the intellectual agility we learn as part of our training in reasoning and analysis [. . .] making words mean what we want them to mean, revising those definitions when they no longer serve our purposes, and formulating and reformulating moral principles accordingly'. Moreover, there is ample empirical evidence that knowledge or intellectual gifts do not protect against biases (see Mercier and Sperber 2018: 214), and evidence that philosophers and ethicists are prone to biased reasoning and post hoc rationalizing (see Schwitzgebel and Ellis 2017: sec. 4.2).

[115] Gregor (1996: 168) translates it as 'are brazen enough to shut their ears to that heavenly voice'. This is less literal, and I think it is important to preserve the term *taub* (see Section 5.2).

philosophers' can make 'doubtful' the question '[w]hat, then, really is *pure* morality, by which as a touchstone one must test the moral content of every action?' (CPrR, V: 155.12–18). However, Kant must be overstating his case here. We have seen that the natural dialectical tension is present within *all* finite rational agents (Section 3.1), not only those exposed to moral theory.[116]

Kant here expresses two main concerns regarding the effect impure practical philosophy can have on agents and on philosophers themselves. First, it can foster *confusion* (see also G, IV: 404.28). Universality and humanity, on the one hand, and philosophical principles, on the other hand, might issue conflicting verdicts and thus make it more difficult to judge correctly. For a confused agent, moral deliberation requires an additional level of intellectual effort to weigh genuine moral concerns against misleading philosophical advice.

Second, impure practical philosophy can make one *deaf* to the voice of reason (see CPrR, V: 35.16–18). 'Deafness' does not mean that the voice of reason itself is silent. Kant believes that his colleagues, even Christian Garve, still hear this voice in their hearts (see Section 5.1). A practical philosopher who is deeply entangled in a false moral theory might not hear the voice of reason qua practical philosopher, but qua rational human being he can still hear it. Adelung (1811: vol. 4, col. 537–8) and Grimm and Grimm (1889: vol. 21, col. 162) note that the German *taub* (deaf) can mean that someone does not *want* to hear or understand something. *Adelung* also notes that deafness can be self-inflicted and intentional. Kant indeed assumes that deafness is self-incurred ('to *make oneself* deaf to that heavenly voice'; CPrR, V: 35.16–18; my emphasis). Deaf agents, even if they were to deliberate based on purely rational criteria – though they are likely also confused and buy into impure principles – conceive of their moral judgement not as an unconditional command, but as merely providing defeasible reasons for actions and as standing in need of external motives. They think that there is no categorical difference between moral commands and counsels of prudence, social mores and so on. When they act from what they take to be their duty, their actions do not exhibit commitment to duty alone.

Confusion and deafness are both aspects of the phenomenon of disregarding purity (see Section 3.2). Confused agents might judge incorrectly about what is morally justified because they have allowed morally irrelevant considerations into their moral deliberations. Deaf agents have false priorities and do not accord duty its proper place. Deafness presupposes some sophisticated

---

[116] Schönecker (1997: 330–2) argues that it is popular practical philosophy that seduces common agents in the first place. However, as should have become clear, it does not take philosophy to become confused. Philosophers are merely better equipped (but not uniquely so) to spread confusion.

theorizing to supposedly justify the diminished status of moral commands. However, this sophisticated theorizing can be disseminated among the less-educated public by educators and public intellectuals. In fact, that is what Kant believes is happening when he laments that the public has a 'taste' (G, IV: 388.25) for popular philosophy.

My discussion raises the question of whether Kant thinks that rationalizing and corruption happens to all of us. Do we all start as innocent common agents, guided by the insights of our common human reason, and rationalize away our grasp of morality? I think that Kant's account is not intended to explain individual development. We are born into a social world already shaped by some of the ideologies Kant warns against. Material for rationalizing is thus already imparted on us during our socialization. Kant's account is highly idealized and rather answers the transcendental question of what the *conditions of the possibility* are for rational agents to falsely deem themselves justified and judge incorrectly about morality, as they sometimes do. For this purpose, Kant discusses agents largely in abstraction from their social surroundings. He believes that the danger of rationalizing is part of the human condition, yet, to understand how individuals under current conditions acquire wrong conceptions of morality, a look at beliefs and values imparted on us by our upbringing and our social surroundings will often afford a more straightforward answer than an idealized story of individual rationalizing.

We should also bear in mind that even though agents are necessarily caught in the natural dialectical tension between their sensuous and rational natures, it is not necessary that agents solve the tension via rationalizing. Agents can refuse to uncritically believe convenient stories that seemingly absolve them of guilt. While most agents are somewhere in between innocence and full corruption, agents can preserve their innocent conception of morality (almost) entirely, if they withstand their propensity to engage in rationalizing. If an agent makes the purity and strictness of the moral law the focal point of her deliberation, she can see through the spuriousness of the considerations her internal lawyer advances.

6 Whose Rationalizing?

Kant's conception of rationalizing allows him to explain why rational agents would find elements of his philosophy 'strange' and express 'suspicion' towards them and his philosophy in general (G, IV: 394.34–5), as he admits they might. He suspects that those who object to his theory aim to devise or defend a conception of morality that is supposed to make more room for their self-interest while allowing them to avoid pangs of conscience and deem themselves worthy of happiness. Having such a response available is important for Kant, because he owes us an explanation for how 'so many people manage to hide from themselves the basic claims of morality' (Ameriks 2000: 150) that, Kant believes, are apparent to everyone.

Moreover, recently Kant's conception of rationalizing was proposed as a systematically attractive response to the overdemandingness objection. Van Ackeren and Sticker (2015: sec. 3) argue that from Kant's perspective levelling an overdemandingness objection against an ethical theory would be a paradigm case of a self-love-driven attack on a fundamental property of morality. In fact, the overdemandingness objection is more overt and brazen than many of the attempts Kant himself discusses. In a standard overdemandingness objection the very notion that morality can demand actions exceeding a supposed threshold of acceptable sacrifice becomes the object of criticism. The rationalizer here starts off with the assumption that there are certain agent-relative goods morality may not interfere with and that this constrains what morality can legitimately demand. This is a straightforward denial of purity.[117]

To assess whether it is fair to criticize the overdemandingness objection as a rationalization, and whether Kant can explain why so many people manage to hide ethical truth from themselves, we must now discuss the philosophical viability of Kant's conception of rationalizing. I begin with an initial problem that Kant can overcome, and then turn to what I take to be the real issue.

As we have seen, rationalizing helps us to understand how rational agents who acknowledge the unconditional authority of morality can come to adopt more lenient moral principles. Furthermore, rationalizing allows Kant to criticize ethical theories, institutions and cultural practices, if they propose and seemingly validate excuses and delegate responsibility to supposed authorities. These cases have in common that agents come to conceive of moral commands as *less* onerous. The driving force behind rationalizing is self-love in a direct form (making space for one's pursuit of happiness) and a more indirect form (avoiding loss of self-esteem and pangs of conscience and deeming oneself worthy of happiness). As an activity driven by self-love, rationalizing can only offer straightforward explanations for why rational agents would take morality to be *less* rather than *more* onerous on them.

While Kant's ethics might be stricter and more demanding than the eudaemonist theories he frequently criticizes, his theory is arguably not the one that is most detrimental to an agent's self-interest. Take, for instance, a form

---

[117] There are also versions of the overdemandingness objection that do not focus on supposed limits of moral demands, and instead criticize how certain ethical theories undermine integrity and agency (Williams 1985) or that moral sainthood is not an ideal fit for humans (Wolf 1982). Kant would presumably also charge these versions with being rationalizations, but the specific mechanisms of rationalizing would be different.

of Act-Consequentialism that postulates a duty to impartially maximize the happiness of all sentient creatures. Such a theory would, in many instances, be extremely demanding on (relatively) affluent agents as it would require that they donate all their resources (up to the point of marginal utility) to charities that effectively help the global poor, victims of natural disasters and maybe also non-rational animals. In addition, they might also have to dedicate their spare time to volunteering and fundraising for these charities or work a second job to make even more money to go towards the maximal promotion of the good. Kant's ethics, by contrast, does not impose demands like these on behalf of others' happiness. At the very least, we can say that beneficence, as an imperfect duty, is trumped by perfect duties and that it has to be balanced with one's duty of self-perfection. In addition, not helping others when one could constitutes lack of merit rather than guilt or vice (MM, VI: 390.18–29),[118] whereas on the Consequentialist theory I sketched it would be morally wrong to do anything short of the maximum.

Now, the question is whether Kant's conception of rationalizing can account for why some rational agents would buy into such a very demanding Consequentialist theory.[119] According to Kant, agents' moral reasoning is tacitly guided by universalizability and the special status of rational agents (see Section 2.3), not by consequences. Moreover, due to the sacrifices impartial maximization would require this notion is not appealing to the self-love of relatively affluent agents, and maybe not even to those not terribly well off, as they would still be forced to view all their decisions through the lens of impartial maximizing ('Is this really the impartially best use I can make of my scarce resources, or could I do more good elsewhere?').[120] Kant's framework seems to lack the means to explain how agents could ever err on the side of more demanding principles or theories, such as impartial Consequentialism.[121]

As a criticism of ethical theories rationalizing puts more demanding moral principles or theories seemingly in a better position than less demanding ones. From the perspective of the more demanding theory we can tell a story as to why

---

[118] See van Ackeren and Sticker (2018) and Formosa and Sticker (2019) for two recent takes on Kantian beneficence stressing that this duty does not require that we do as much as we can. Even on a more demanding reading of imperfect duties (as, for instance, presented by Timmermann 2018), beneficence would still be constrained by other duties.

[119] Of course, it could be the case that impartial Consequentialism is the right ethical theory, instead of the product of rationalizing. I discuss this below.

[120] See Railton's (1984) and Williams's (1973) prominent cases against standard Consequentialism.

[121] It should be noted that some thinkers with whom Kant was familiar acknowledged that conscience can be overly strict or *scrupulöse* (Crusius 1772: §46, 184–6). Such thinkers would be able to account for the existence of incorrect and yet overly demanding conceptions of morality.

the less demanding theories or principles originated in rationalizing rather than unbiased inquiry, but not vice versa. However, the mere fact that a theory is highly demanding does not make this theory more defensible. Even Kant, who is frequently criticized for supposed excessive rigorism, agrees with this. He criticizes the 'fantastically virtuous who allows *nothing to be morally indifferent* (*adiaphora*) and strews all his steps with duties, as with mantraps'. 'Fantastic virtue' can even 'turn the government of virtue into tyranny' (MM, VI: 409.13–19). He also praises the Epicurean idea of an 'ever-cheerful heart' (MM, VI: 485.5) as an important part of a moral life and criticizes the Stoics for straining 'the moral capacity of the *human being*, under the name of a *sage*, far beyond all the limits of his human nature' (CPrR, V: 127.2–4).[122] Kant does not think that between two courses of action the one that is more detrimental to one's self-love must be the morally correct one. It should thus not be the case that the more demanding theory is automatically more defensible than the less demanding theory, even though this is what seemingly follows from Kant's conception of rationalizing.[123] However, while agents typically err on the side of their self-love, it is perfectly conceivable (and can be observed in everyday life) that agents are too hard on themselves and can feel compelled to do more than what can reasonably be expected of them or feel guilty for failing to do so.[124] Rationalizing, it seems, cannot account for this aspect of our moral (mis)judgements.

To see whether there is a way out for Kant, we need to look at his conception of self-love. According to the Second Critique's Theorem II, all material, that is, non-moral, principles and ends, 'come under the general principle of self-love or one's own happiness' (CPrR, V: 22.6–8; see also CPrR, V: 34.2–11, 35.7–11). Anything that is not motivated by respect for the moral law is thus self-love-driven. The corresponding theory of non-moral and immoral actions has been the target of heated criticism, as it is often considered to represent an overly simplistic form of hedonism concerning non-moral actions.[125]

---

[122] Moreover, Vogt (2008) argues that Kant's ethics is much less restrictive than many believe, since duties to self make room within morality for agents to pursue their personal projects. Herman (2011: 100) argues that obligatory ends 'bring a wide range of ordinary human concerns inside morality'. There is widespread agreement in the Kant literature that the idea that Kant's ethics is one of austerity and self-abnegation is a caricature.

[123] That rationalizing falls short as a general explanation for why agents would adopt principles that appear incorrect from a Kantian perspective (including more demanding principles) is also highlighted as a problem by Papish (2018: 235).

[124] See, for instance, MacFarquhar's (2016) descriptions of the lives of contemporary 'moral saints' who live extraordinarily moral lives, dedicated to the poor, orphans, animal welfare etc.

[125] See, for instance, Beck (1960: 92–102) and Williams (1985: 64). See also Reath (2006: 34–5): 'Kant's scheme appears to leave no room for ends of personal importance to the agent, whose originating motive is not the sense of duty: activities and goals of personal interest, career interests, friendships and personal relationships, devotion to family, and so on. If we do try to fit

However, according to Kant, agents can adopt *other-directed* ends. Some of these are obligatory ends, such as others' happiness, whereas others fall under *self-love*; the friend of humanity is 'attuned to compassion' and finds 'even without another motivating ground of vanity, or self-interest [...] an inner gratification in spreading joy around them' (G, IV: 398.9–12; see also CPrR, V: 35.37–8). Kant clearly 'recognizes that we can have inclinations that are straightforwardly other-regarding' (Reath 2006: 49).[126] Moreover, 'Kant recognizes a category of inclinations that develop from a natural "aptitude for culture", whose objects include pursuits in the arts and sciences or the increase of one's knowledge, as well as social values or goods' (Reath 2006: 39–40; see also CJ, V: 429–34). The object of these inclinations is not pleasure and these inclinations should not be understood as egoistic, even though they are self-directed.

We thus must distinguish self-love from self-interest or egoism in a narrow, self-directed sense. It is possible that agents adopt among their personal ends other-directed ends, such as philanthropy or altruism, and that they promote these ends even at the expense of other personal and self-directed ends. Agents might adopt these other-directed ends for a number of reasons. They might consider them a source of personal satisfaction; they might think that these ends supplement and complement other ends they hold; people they admire might care about these ends. Ends such as philanthropy and altruism, even though they require sacrifices in terms of self-directed ends, can thus fall under self-love. In fact, Kant is very clear that acts of charity do not necessarily reflect a good moral disposition but might rather be purely emotional or pathological responses driven by self-love (G, IV: 398.8–399.2).

Of course, philanthropy and altruism can also be genuinely moral, that is, non-self-love-driven. Agents might interpret their duty to make others' ends their own as morally requiring acts of philanthropy or charity and adopt corresponding principles for *moral* reasons. Other, more demanding principles such as doing as much good as possible are somewhat more difficult to capture as part of a Kantian imperfect duty, though, since Kant would presumably maintain that it is the maxim and motivation that is important, not the *outcomes*

---

such ends into this classification, we must take them to be motivated by the desire for pleasure. Here Kant would seem to face two unattractive alternatives. Either his scheme ignores many ordinary activities that give value and substance to life, in which case it seems radically incomplete. Or it includes them by forcing them into a hedonistic mold that is inappropriate [...] that fails to acknowledge differences in the value and importance of the many different kinds of activities grouped together.'

[126] It is a standard rebuttal of psychological hedonism, dating back to Joseph Butler, 'that it confuses the object of a desire with the satisfaction that will result when that object is attained. [...] The desire may have a cause that is independent of the satisfaction that results in its fulfilment, and may be directed at an end outside of the self' (Reath 2006: 37).

of actions.[127] Yet, it seems that a maxim of helping when and where one can do most (or much) good could in principle fall under imperfect duties to others.[128]

Depending on the grounds for adopting philanthropy and altruism, these ends can either fall under self-love or under the duty of beneficence. In the latter case, these ends are not the result of rationalizing but simply constitute one way to fulfil one's imperfect duties to others. In the former case, rationalizing might serve to make more room for the promotion of these ends, since self-love is not restricted to self-directed or egoistic ends. Presenting apparent justifications and excuses for promoting personal but other-directed ends is rationalizing, if there is a danger that agents will neglect duties, such as self-perfection, or even come to believe that perfect duties admit of exceptions, for instance, for the sake of acquiring more money to donate to charity. This can transform agents' original grasp of morality in much the same way as making excuses for one's self-directed ends can; the agent might deem themselves excused or even fully justified because they acted for a supposed higher good, and they might, in the future, apply similar considerations to assessment of themselves and others. Moreover, they might come to believe that even perfect duties can and should be ignored in certain cases and must be weighed against other factors such as the consequences of actions.[129]

Rationalizers can come to adopt and defend principles of altruism that demand more than the imperfect duty of beneficence does and that might even interfere with morality. Such rationalizing is still self-love-driven insofar as agents aim to make more space for one of their *personal*, albeit other-directed, ends at the expense of duty. This form of rationalizing is in some senses similar to the eudaemonist (Section 3.3) who starts off as someone who greatly values morality and cannot face the prospect of not living up to his rational self. Adopting demanding principles of philanthropy or altruism, and making morality supposedly more demanding than it really is, is tempting in the sense that an agent does not engage in a crude attempt to make space for selfishness. Rather, it seems that they hold themselves to higher standards than others. This, however, misses the crucial point that there is one and the same moral standard for everyone, pure practical reason, and that it is dangerous to tamper with this standard and to think that one knows better than reason.

---

[127] In fact, Kant emphasizes that 'the virtue is greater when the benefactor's means are limited' (MM, VI: 453.30–1), not when the benefactor does more good, though sometimes Kant does stress the importance of both obstacles or sacrifices on the part of the agent and how much good could be done (MM, VI: 228.16–17).

[128] Kant himself sometimes indicates that fulfilling our imperfect duties can be very demanding; it is an agent's 'duty at each instant [...] to do all the good in his power' (Rel, VI: 72.11), '[t]o be beneficent where one can is one's duty' (G, IV: 398.8) and an agent should 'try, as far as he can, to advance the ends of others' (G, IV: 430.21–7).

[129] My discussion of philanthropy and altruism here is *pars pro toto* for non-self-directed and potentially costly ends such as animal welfare, political activism etc.

Finally, we might also wonder whether philanthropy or altruism can be an object of rationalizing if an agent adopted them *from duty* as part of their obligatory end of furthering others' happiness. For instance, what if an agent always prioritizes these aspects of their imperfect duties over their self-perfection or even over perfect duty? Since I have assumed throughout my investigation that rationalizing is driven by self-love, I have to deny that such a mistaken prioritization can be the outcome of rationalizing, if an agent is really committed to philanthropy and altruism on *moral* grounds. We should bear in mind, though, that not all mistakes an agent makes have to be the outcome of rationalizing as I described it. An agent might make honest mistakes[130] when prioritizing certain duties over others and Kant would presumably think them blameless if they are genuinely committed to duty and seek to earnestly follow the guidance afforded by universalization tests and the special status of rational nature.

One might very well wonder at this point: isn't it a good thing to do more good for others rather than less? In what sense would an agent who dedicates their life to helping the worst-off be a rationalizer at all, even if they make morality more demanding on them than universality and rational nature prescribe? They might be acting out of self-love in a wide and technical sense. However, as we have seen, self-love is not necessarily a form of egoism but a structure that motivates an agent to act on personal ends that they have adopted possibly as the result of earnest and critical reflection. Could Kantian theory, if it criticizes as a rationalizing transformation of morality the command to do as much good for others as one can, be the real rationalization that plays down the true extent of our obligations to the worst-off?[131]

---

[130] The category of honest mistakes might strike Kantians as odd, given Kant's great optimism concerning matters of moral epistemology (see Section 2.3). What I have in mind here is not a mistake about what duties we have in the first place, but an incorrect prioritization among various of our duties that might apply to one and the same specific situation. For instance, an agent might be faced with a situation where they could substantially improve the plight of the poor by stealing property and giving it to the poor. It seems to me that if an agent is moved to steal due to otherwise morally admirable character traits, such as commitment to the welfare of the worst-off and/or compassion, and the agent is genuinely convinced that stealing is what they have to do in this situation, then it would be odd to say that they acted from self-love. Rather, from a Kantian perspective, they made a mistake (violating property laws/perfect duties), albeit an honest one because the mistake constituted an exercise of otherwise morally admirable character traits and responded to morally relevant features of the situation. I should also say that nothing in my conception of rationalizing hinges on the existence of these honest mistakes. Incorrect prioritization of duties falls outside of the scope of my framework, but it is potentially a significant field of mistakes or at least of sub-optimal moral behaviour that often gets overlooked in Kant scholarship due to the assumption that whenever our actions deviate from moral norms the underlying explanation must be self-love.

[131] As I pointed out, Kant could in principle accept extremely demanding rescue and aid principles as ways of implementing imperfect duties to others. However, Kant would certainly not want these principles to eclipse all other obligations, especially not perfect duties (such as prohibitions against fraudulently obtaining money to give to charity). The contentious point between

This is not a moot challenge. After all, ethical theories other than Kant's can come up with their very own theory of rationalizing. For instance, Consequentialists might want to describe as idle rationalizing all philosophizing about who or what really is responsible for causing an emergency situation or ongoing absolute poverty (consumers, corporations, capitalism etc.) and for alleviating it (those who caused it, those who benefit etc.), when there is an acute need that *you* could alleviate and no one else is doing enough. It is, according to most Consequentialists, clearly you who ought to act in this situation. Fundamental questions concerning who is to blame for creating this situation are potentially distracting, and must come second. Moreover, Consequentialists might level a rationalizing charge specifically against Kant, because his philosophy suggests that we have latitude concerning some duties that might be a matter of life and death for victims of natural disasters and the global poor,[132] and that inflexible absolute prohibitions might unduly restrain our actions in acute emergencies.[133]

This reveals the real problem for Kant's conception of rationalizing: how can Kant be certain that it is not he who is the rationalizer who, in his heart, knows that he and everyone else must maximize overall happiness (or maybe strive for personal eudaemonia) but whose head has convinced him otherwise? Or, more generally: how can we identify rationalizing without already making substantive and controversial assumptions about what correct moral reasoning is?[134] After all, if rationalizing is to be a plausible explanation for the existence of (widespread) beliefs that deviate from the correct ethical theory (whatever this theory might be), then we need *theory-independent* criteria for what counts as rationalizing, not criteria based on contentious features of morality. Only criteria remaining neutral regarding the specific content of the correct ethical theory can adjudicate between the Kantian and Consequentialists (and other theorists) when they accuse each other of rationalizing. These criteria would provide a philosopher with the opportunity to critically diagnose moral

---

Kant and the Consequentialist would still be what the status and stringency of a 'Help/Do as much as you can' principle is, and whether this is the only adequate principle of beneficence that an agent could commit to.

[132] Stohr (2011: 46) points out that Utilitarians could criticize Kant and Kantian ethics for not being 'adequately demanding when it comes to beneficence'. Moreover, Schwitzgebel and Ellis (2017: 181) suggest that Kant's views on masturbation and the rights of women and children born out of wedlock are the product of prudishness, sexism and homophobia and that the supposed reasons he provides for these views are rationalizations.

[133] See Pinheiro Walla (2015) for discussion of the resources Kant has available to deal with rescue cases involving rights violations, such as using someone else's property without permission to rescue a person in need.

[134] Schwitzgebel and Ellis (2017: 176) make the very astute observation that 'leaping quickly to the assumption that other people are rationalizing can itself be a kind of rationalizing justification for dismissing their views'.

reasoning by picking out features that should be suspicious on any plausible moral theory. I can here only hint at what such criteria might look like.

One plausible theory-independent criterion is *consistency across principles*. It should make us suspicious if an agent switches between ethical principles in such a way that their interests always 'happen' to be favoured, for example, the agent is a latitudinarian about their duties to those worse off than them, but an Act-Consequentialist when the impartial perspective of the universe would favour their own happiness.[135] Behaviour like this should strike anyone as suspect (unless, of course, the agent can provide a plausible rationale for why different ethical theories or principles must be combined in the way they do), and indicates rationalizing. Consistency across principles can help us spot particularly egregious misuses of rational capacities. This criterion alone, however, is too thin to pick out many of the more sophisticated forms of rationalizing, given that reasoning that consistently sticks to just one or a few principles can still be false. Presumably, there are many false ethical theories that do not wildly jump between principles.

A second criterion is *hypocrisy*, inconsistency between the standards an agent professes to hold and the standards they act on, or between the standards they use to evaluate themselves and those they use to evaluate others. Again, avoiding hypocrisy is a rather basic requirement. In addition, it might of course be true that different areas (politics, business, the private sphere) call for different standards of assessment and all kinds of dicey issues can arise concerning the question of which cases and situations are alike and call for being adjudicated according to the same principles.[136]

Generally, we should be suspicious if an agent's self-interest always seems to come out on top. However, as I argued, we should certainly not dismiss an ethical theory simply because it is not maximally detrimental to an agent's wellbeing. How demanding morality should be is a substantive question that cannot be settled by discussions of rationalizing. This makes it difficult to evaluate whether someone is a rationalizer based on just one or a few judgements. Rather, we have to look at patterns of judgements and see whether an agent employs the same principles consistently, and whether these principles are

---

[135] Another example is that I personally find myself to be much more of a Marxist – and so sceptical of the very possibility of 'fair trade' – every time I find myself confronted with the higher price of fair-trade products, whereas I am much less of a Marxist when it comes to my own private property.

[136] In addition, for some ethical approaches, such as so-called 'Government House Consequentialism', it is legitimate and maybe even required to publicly advocate a theory that one privately does not endorse, because this would be what foreseeably maximizes the good (see Parfit 1986: sec. 17). It is not clear that this should count as hypocrisy if the agent is also willing to be deceived by others if this, overall, makes things go best.

such that they seem to make room for the agent's own desires and personal pursuits to an extent that should be suspicious no matter what specific theory we buy into.

A third theory-independent criterion that indicates rationalizing is if an agent exhibits *confirmation or myside bias* by never considering objections and only ever looking for arguments and reasons supporting their own position. This, once more, is a pattern and not something we can identify in a single judgement. Moreover, even if we notice such a pattern, we have to be careful. Just because an agent does not consider objections does not mean that the conclusion of their reasoning is wrong. They could get it right by chance. Their reasoning is, however, at least suspicious.

It would be fruitful to think more about these and potentially other theory-independent criteria for rationalizing in order to understand the plausibility of the charge of rationalizing – against eudaemonism, impartial Consequentialism and Kant himself. I hope to have at least demonstrated why working this out would be a desideratum for our understanding of rationalizing, as well as for working out *who* rationalizes: Kant's critics, Kant himself, neither or both?

Abbreviations

Kant's writings are cited by volume: page.line of the Academy edition, using the following abbreviations.

A/B:	*Critique of Pure Reason*
Anth:	*Anthropology from a Pragmatic Point of View*
CPrR:	*Critique of Practical Reason*
CJ:	*Critique of Judgement*
CF:	*The Contest of Faculties*
CB:	*Conjectural Beginning of Human History*
TP:	*On the Common Saying: That may be correct in theory, but it is of no use in practice*
OAD:	*On a Discovery, according to which any new Critique of Pure Reason is made Superfluous through an Older*
WIE:	*Answering the Question: What is Enlightenment*
FI:	*First Introduction to the Critique of Judgement*
G:	*Groundwork of the Metaphysics of Morals*
JL:	*Immanuel Kant's Logic: A manual for lectures edited by Gottlob Benjamin Jäsche*
LB-Prog:	*Lose Blätter zu den Fortschritten der Metaphysik*
Eth-C:	*Moral Philosophy: Collin's Lecture Notes*
Corr:	*Letters*
L-F:	*Die Vorlesungen des Wintersemesters 1775/76 aufgrund der Nachschriften Friedländer 3.3 (Ms 400), Friedländer 2 (Ms 399) und Prieger*
Eth-K:	*Kaehler's Lecture Notes on Moral Philosophy*, edited by Stark (2004)
Eth-M1:	*Lecture Notes Mrongovius 1*
Eth-M2:	*Morality according to Prof. Kant: Mrongovius's second set of lecture notes*
L-Men:	*Die Vorlesung des Wintersemesters 1781/82 [?] aufgrund der Nachschriften Menschenkunde, Petersburg*
Eth-P:	*Praktische Philosophie Powalski*
Eth-V:	*Metaphysics of Morals Vigilantius*
MM:	*The Metaphysics of Morals*
Men:	*Einige Bermekungen zu Ludwig Heinrich Jakob's Prüfung der Mendelsohn'schen Morgenstunden*
MFNS:	*Metaphysical Foundations of Natural Science*

OP:	*Opus postumum*
P:	*Prolegomena to any Future Metaphysics*
Ped:	*On Pedagogy*
P-F:	*Preparations for The Contest of Faculties*
P-M:	*Preparations for The Metaphysics of Morals*
TPP:	*Toward Perpetual Peace*
P-PR:	*Vorredenentwürfe Religionsphilosophie*
PCT:	*Verkündigung des nahen Abschlusses eines Tractats zum ewigen Frieden in der Philosophie*
PM:	*Prize Essay on the Progress of Metaphysics*
Rel:	*Religion within the Limits of Reason Alone*
Ref:	*Reflections on Anthropology*
RE:	*Zur Rezension von Eberhards Magazin (II. Band)*
Ref:	*Reflections*
RO:	*Remarks on the Observations on the Feeling of the Beautiful and the Sublime*
RPT:	*On a New Superior Tone in Philosophy*
UPT:	*On the Use of Teleological Principles in Philosophy*
MPT:	*Miscarriages of all Philosophical Trials in Theodicy*

Unless otherwise noted, translations follow the *Cambridge Edition of the Works of Immanuel Kant*, edited by P. Guyer and A. W. Wood (1992ff.). Translations of as-yet-untranslated passages and of German secondary literature are my own.

References

Adelung, Johann Christoph (1811) *Grammatisch-kritisches Wörterbuch der hochdeutschen Mundart* (Vienna: Bauer).

Allais, Lucy (2021) 'Deceptive Unity and Productive Disunity: Kant's Account of Situated Moral Selves'. In Ansgar Lyssy and Christopher Yeomans (eds.), *Dimensions of Normativity in Kant* (London: Palgrave), pp. 45–67.

Allison, Henry (1990) *Kant's Theory of Freedom* (Cambridge: Cambridge University Press).

(2011) *Kant's* Groundwork of the Metaphysics of Morals: *A Commentary* (Oxford, New York: Oxford University Press).

Ameriks, Karl (2000) *The Fate of Autonomy: Problems in the Appropriation of the Critical Philosophy* (Cambridge: Cambridge University Press).

(2003) *Interpreting Kant's Critiques* (Oxford, New York: Oxford University Press).

(2012) *Kant's Elliptical Path* (Oxford: Oxford University Press).

Anderson, Elizabeth (2016) 'The Social Epistemology of Morality: Learning from the Forgotten History of the Abolition of Slavery'. In Michael Brady and Miranda Fricker (eds.), *The Epistemic Life of Groups: Essays in the Epistemology of Collectives* (Oxford: Oxford University Press), pp. 75–94.

Bacin, Stefano (2013) 'The Perfect Duty to Oneself Merely as a Moral Being (TL 6: 428–437)'. In Andreas Trampota, Oliver Sensen and Jens Timmermann (eds.), *Kant's 'Tugendlehre': A Comprehensive Commentary* (Berlin, Boston, MA: De Gruyter), pp. 245–69.

Baron, Marcia (2005) '(Putative) Justification'. *Annual Review of Law and Ethics*, 13, 377–94.

(2007) 'Excuses, Excuses'. *Criminal Law and Philosophy*, 1(1), 21–39.

Beck, Lewis White (1960) *A Commentary on Kant's Critique of Practical Reason* (Chicago, IL: University of Chicago Press).

Broadie, Alexander and Pybus, Elizabeth (1982) 'Kant and Weakness of Will'. *Kant-Studien*, 73(4), 406–11.

Callanan, John (2019) 'Kant on Misology and the Natural Dialectic'. *Philosophers' Imprint*, 19(47), 1–22.

Caswell, Matthew (2006) 'The Value of Humanity and Kant's Conception of Evil'. *Journal of the History of Philosophy*, 44(4), 635–63.

Caygill, Howard (1995) *A Kant Dictionary* (Cambridge, MA: Blackwell).

Cohen, Alix (2020) 'A Kantian Account of Emotions as Feelings'. *Mind*, 129 (514), 429–60.

Crusius, Christian (1772) *Kurzer Begriff der Moraltheologie, oder nähere Erklärung der praktischen Lehren des Christentums* (Leipzig: Ulrich Christian Saalbach).

Cushman, Fiery (2020) 'Rationalization is Rational'. *Behavioral and Brain Sciences*, 43(28), 1–16.

Darwall, Stephen L. (1988) 'Self-Deception, Autonomy, and Moral Constitution'. In Brian McLaughlin and Amelie Rorty (eds.), *Perspectives on Self-Deception* (Berkeley: University of California Press), pp. 407–31.

Di Giulio, Sara (2020) '*Video meliora proboque, deteriora sequor.* Zur Irreführung des Gewissens bei Kant'. In Sara Di Giulio and Alberto Frigo (eds.), *Kasuistik und Theorie des Gewissens. Von Pascal bis Kant* (Berlin: De Gruyter), pp. 233–89.

Eisler, Rudolf (1930) *Kant-Lexikon. Nachschlagewerk zu Kants sämtlichen Schriften/Briefen und Handschriftlichem Nachlass* (Berlin: Pan-Verlag Kurt Metzner).

Ellis, Jonathan and Schwitzgebel, Eric (2020) 'Rationalization in the Pejorative Sense: Cushman's Account Overlooks the Scope and Costs of Rationalization'. *Behavioral and Brain Sciences*, 43(28), 23–4.

Formosa, Paul (2009) 'Kant on the Limits of Human Evil'. *Journal of Philosophical Research*, 34, 189–214.

  (2017) *Kantian Ethics, Dignity and Perfection* (Cambridge: Cambridge University Press).

Formosa, Paul and Sticker, Martin (2019) 'Kant and the Demandingness of the Virtue of Beneficence'. *European Journal of Philosophy*, 27(3), 625–42.

Franklin, Benjamin (1909) *The Life of Benjamin Franklin: An Autographical Manuscript* (New York: P.F. Collier and Son).

Freyenhagen, Fabian (2011) 'Empty, Useless, and Dangerous? Recent Kantian Replies to the Empty Formalism Objection'. *Hegel Bulletin*, 32(1–2), 95–118.

Frierson, Patrick (2014) *Kant's Empirical Psychology* (Cambridge: Cambridge University Press).

Graham, Jesse (2020) 'Ideology, Shared Moral Narratives, and the Dark Side of Collective Rationalization'. *Behavioral and Brain Sciences*, 43 (28), 24–5.

Gregor, Mary J. (1996) *Practical Philosophy (The Cambridge Edition of the Works of Immanuel Kant in Translation)* (Cambridge: Cambridge University Press).

Grenberg, Jeanine (2010) 'What is the Enemy of Virtue?'. In Lara Denis (ed.), *Kant's* Metaphysics of Morals: *A Critical Guide* (Cambridge: Cambridge University Press), pp. 152–70.

(2013) *Kant's Defense of Common Moral Experience. A Phenomenological Account* (Cambridge: Cambridge University Press).

Grimm, Jacob and Grimm, Willhelm (1889) *Deutsches Wörterbuch von Jacob Grimm und Wilhelm Grimm* (Leipzig: Hirzel). Available at http://dwb.uni-trier.de/de/.

Guyer, Paul (2000) *Kant on Freedom, Law, and Happiness* (Cambridge: Cambridge University Press).

(2003) 'Kant on Common Sense and Scepticism'. *Kantian Review*, 7(1), 1–38.

Guyer, Paul and Matthews, Eric (2000) *Critique of the Power of Judgment (The Cambridge Edition of the Works of Immanuel Kant in Translation)* (Cambridge: Cambridge University Press).

Guyer, Paul and Wood, Allen (1992ff.) *Cambridge Edition of the Works of Immanuel Kant* (Cambridge: Cambridge University Press).

(1998) *Critique of Pure Reason (The Cambridge Edition of the Works of Immanuel Kant in Translation)* (Cambridge: Cambridge University Press).

Haidt, Jonathan (2001) 'The Emotional Dog and its Rational Tail: A Social Intuitionist Approach to Moral Judgment'. *Psychological Review*, 108(4), 814–34.

Henrich, Dieter (1967) *Kant: Gentz. Rehberg. Über Theorie und Praxis* (Frankfurt a. M.: Suhrkamp).

(1994) *Dieter Henrich. The Unity of Reason: Essays on Kant's Philosophy*, ed. Richard Velkley (Cambridge, MA: Harvard University Press).

Herman, Barbara (2011) 'A Mismatch of Methods'. In Derek Parfit (ed.), *On What Matters*, vol. 2 (Oxford: Oxford University Press), pp. 83–116.

Herodotus (n.d.) *The History of Herodotus*, trans. George Rawlinson. http://classics.mit.edu/Herodotus/history.html.

Hill, Thomas E., Jr. (2012) *Virtue, Rules, and Justice: Kantian Aspirations* (Oxford: Oxford University Press).

Hill, Thomas E., Jr. and Boxill, Bernard (2001) 'Kant and Race'. In Bernard Boxill (ed.), *Race and Racism* (New York: Oxford University Press), pp. 448–71.

Holzhey, Helmut and Mudroch, Vilem (2005) *Historical Dictionary of Kant and Kantianism* (Lanham, MD: The Scarecrow Press).

Kemp Smith, Norman (1933) *The Critique of Pure Reason* (London: Macmillan).

Kerstein, Samuel (2002) *Kant's Search for the Supreme Principle of Morality* (Cambridge: Cambridge University Press).

Klingner, Stefan (2012) *Technische Vernunft. Kants Zweckbegriff und das Problem einer Philosophie der technischen Kultur* (Berlin, Boston, MA: De Gruyter).

Kohl, Markus (2017a) 'Radical Evil as a Regulative Idea'. *Journal of the History of Philosophy*, 55(4), 641–73.

(2017b) 'The Normativity of Prudence'. *Kant-Studien*, 108(4), 517–42.

Korsgaard, Christine (2009) *Self-Constitution: Agency, Identity, and Integrity* (Oxford: Oxford University Press).

Kuehn, Manfred (2001) *Kant. A Biography* (Cambridge: Cambridge University Press).

MacFarquar, Larissa (2016) *Strangers Drowning: Voyages to the Brink of Moral* Extremity (London: Penguin).

Mele, Alfred (1987) *Irrationality: An Essay on Akrasia, Self-Deception, and Self-Control* (New York, Oxford: Oxford University Press).

Mercier, Hugo and Sperber, Dan (2018) *The Enigma of Reason: A New Theory of Human Understanding* (London: Penguin).

Moeller, Sophie (2020) *Kant's Tribunal of Reason* (Cambridge: Cambridge University Press).

Moran, Kate (2014) 'Delusions of Virtue: Kant on Self-Conceit'. *Kantian Review*, 19(3), 445–73.

Morrisson, Iain (2005) 'On Kantian Maxims: A Reconciliation of the Incorporation Thesis and Weakness of the Will'. *History of Philosophy Quarterly*, 22(1), 73–89.

Musil, Robert (1930) *Der Mann ohne Eigenschaften* (Hamburg: Rowohlt).

Papish, Laura (2018) *Kant on Evil, Self-Deception, and Moral Reform* (Oxford: Oxford University Press).

Parfit, Derek (1986) *Reasons and Persons* (Oxford: Oxford University Press).

Pinheiro Walla, Alice (2015) 'Kant's Moral Theory and Demandingness'. *Ethical Theory and Moral Practice*, 18(4), 731–43.

Piper, Adrian (1987) 'Moral Theory and Moral Alienation'. *Journal of Philosophy*, 84(2), 102–18.

(1988) 'Pseudorationality'. In Brian McLaughlin and Amelie Rorty (eds.), *Perspectives on Self-Deception* (Berkeley: University of California Press), pp. 297–324.

(2008) *Rationality and the Structure of the Self. Volume II: A Kantian Conception*. Available at: www.adrianpiper.com/rss/docs/PiperRSSVol2KC .pdf.

(2012a) 'Kant's Self-Legislation Procedure Reconsidered'. *Kant Studies Online*, 203–77.

(2012b) 'Kant's Two Solutions to the Free Rider Problem'. *Kant Yearbook*, 4, 114–42.

Potter, Nelson (2002) 'Duties to Oneself, Motivational Internalism and Self-Deception'. In Mark Timmons (ed.), *Kant's 'Metaphysics of Morals': Interpretative Essays* (Oxford: Oxford University Press), pp. 371–90.

Railton, Peter (1984) 'Alienation, Consequentialism, and the Demands of Morality'. *Philosophy and Public Affairs*, 13(2), 134–71.

(1986) 'Moral Realism'. *Philosophical Review*, 95(2), 163–207.

Reath, Andrews (2006) *Agency and Autonomy in Kant's Moral Theory: Selected Essays* (Oxford: Oxford University Press).

Rochefoucauld, Francois de la (2002) *Réflexions ou sentences et maximes morales et réflexions diverses*, édition établie et présentée par Laurence Plazenet (Paris: Honoré Champion).

Rukgaber, Matthew (2015) 'Irrationality and Self-Deception within Kant's Grades of Evil'. *Kant-Studien*, 106(2), 234–58.

Scanlon, T. M. (2011) 'How I Am Not a Kantian'. In Derek Parfit (ed.), *On What Matters*, vol. 2 (Oxford: Oxford University Press), pp. 116–39.

Schapiro, Tamar (2006) 'Kantian Rigorism and Mitigating Circumstances'. *Ethics*, 117(1), 32–57.

Schönecker, Dieter (1997) 'Gemeine sittliche und philosophische Vernunfterkenntnis. Zum ersten Übergang in Kants *Grundlegung*'. *Kant-Studien*, 88(3), 311–33.

Schwitzgebel, Eric and Ellis, Jonathan (2017) 'Rationalization in Moral and Philosophical Thought'. In Jean-François Bonnefon and Bastien Tremoliere (eds.), *Moral Inferences* (London: Psychology Press), pp. 170–91.

Sedgwick, Sally (2008) *Kant's* Groundwork of the Metaphysics of Morals: *An Introduction* (Cambridge: Cambridge University Press).

Sensen, Oliver (2013) 'The Moral Importance of Autonomy'. In Oliver Sensen (ed.), *Kant on Moral Autonomy* (Cambridge: Cambridge University Press), pp. 262–81.

(2014) 'Universalizing as a Moral Demand'. *Estudos Kantianos*, 2(1), 169–84.

Seymour Fahmy, Melissa (2019) 'On Virtues of Love and Wide Ethical Duties'. *Kantian Review*, 24(3), 415–37.

Shell, Susan (2009) *Kant and the Limits of Autonomy* (Cambridge, MA: Harvard University Press).

Sherman, Nancy (1997) *Making a Necessity of Virtue: Aristotle and Kant on Virtue* (Cambridge: Cambridge University Press).

Sidgwick, Henry (1907) *Three Methods of Ethics* (London: Macmillan).

Sievers, Thomas (2020) 'Antecedent Rationalization: Rationalization Prior to Action'. *Behavioral and Brain Sciences*, 43(28), 34–5.

Sorensen, Roy A. (1985) 'Self-Deception and Scattered Events'. *Mind*, 94 (373), 64–9.

Stark, Werner (ed.) (2004) *Immanuel Kant. Vorlesung zur Moralphilosophie* (Berlin, New York: De Gruyter).

Sticker, Martin (2015) 'The Moral-Psychology of the Common Agent – A Reply to Ido Geiger'. *British Journal for the History of Philosophy*, 23 (5), 976–89.

(2016a) 'When the Reflective Watch-Dog Barks – Conscience and Self-Deception in Kant'. *The Journal of Value Inquiry*, 51(1), 85–104.

(2016b) 'Kant on Engaging Other Agents and Observing Reason at Work'. *History of Philosophy Quarterly*, 33(4), 347–73.

(2017a) 'Kant's Criticism of Common Moral Rational Cognition'. *European Journal of Philosophy*, 25(1), 85–109.

(2017b) 'Experiments in Ethics? Kant on Chemistry, Means of Education and Methods of Practical Philosophy'. *Idealistic Studies*, 46(1), 41–63.

(2020a) 'Kant und das fehlbare Gewissen'. In Sara Di Giulio and Alberto Frigo (eds.), *Kasuistik und Theorie des Gewissens. Von Pascal bis Kant* (Berlin: De Gruyter), pp. 289–311.

(2020b) 'Kant, Eudaimonism, Act-Consequentialism and the Fact of Reason'. *Archiv für Geschichte der Philosophie*, 102(2), 209–41.

(2021a) 'How Common is Common Human Reason? The Plurality of Moral Perspectives and Kant's Ethics'. In Ansgar Lyssy and Christopher Yeomans (eds.), *Dimensions of Normativity in Kant* (London: Palgrave), pp. 167–89.

(2021b) 'Kant, Moral Overdemandingness and Self-Scrutiny'. *NOUS*, 25(2), 293–316.

Stohr, Karen (2011) 'Kantian Beneficence and the Problem of Obligatory Aid'. *Journal of Moral Philosophy*, 8(1), 45–67.

Timmermann, Jens (2007) *Kant's* Groundwork of the Metaphysics of Morals: *A Commentary* (Cambridge: Cambridge University Press).

(2011) *Groundwork of the Metaphysics of Morals*, trans. Jens Timmermann and Mary Gregor (Cambridge: Cambridge University Press).

(2018) 'Autonomy, Progress and Virtue: Why Kant Has Nothing to Fear from the Overdemandingness Objection'. *Kantian Review*, 23(3), 379–97.

(2020) 'Der Status unvollkommener Pflichten in Kants Theorie des Gewissens'. In Sara Di Giulio and Alberto Frigo (eds.), *Kasuistik und Theorie des Gewissens. Von Pascal bis Kant* (Berlin: De Gruyter), pp. 217–33.

Van Ackeren, Marcel and Sticker, Martin (2015) 'Kant on Moral Demandingness'. *Ethical Theory and Moral Practice*, 18(1), 75–89.

(2018) 'Moral Rationalism and Demandingness in Kant'. *Kantian Review*, 23 (3), 407–28.

Vogt, Katja (2008) 'Duties to Others: Demands and Limits'. In Monika Betzler (ed.), *Kant's Virtue Ethics* (Berlin, New York: De Gruyter), pp. 219–45.

Vujosevic, Marijana (2018) 'Kant's Account of Moral Weakness'. *European Journal of Philosophy*. http://doi.org/10.1111/ejop.12389.

Ware, Owen (2009) 'The Duty of Self-Knowledge'. *Philosophy and Phenomenological Research*, 79(3), 671–98.

(2021) *Kant's Justification of Ethics* (Oxford: Oxford University Press).

Wehofsits, Anna (2016) *Anthropologie und Moral. Affekte, Leidenschaften und Mitgefühl in Kants Ethik* (Berlin: De Gruyter).

(2020) 'Passions: Kant's Psychology of Self-Deception'. *Inquiry*. http://doi.org/10.1080/0020174X.2020.1801498.

Welsch, Martin (2019) 'Kant über den Selbstbetrug des Bösen'. *Kant-Studien*, 110(1), 49–73.

Willaschek, Marcus, Stolzenberg, Jürgen, Mohr, Georg and Bacin, Stefano (eds.) (2015) *Kant-Lexikon* (Berlin, Boston, MA: De Gruyter).

Williams, Bernard (1973) *Utilitarianism: For and Against*, with J. J. C. Smart (Cambridge: Cambridge University Press).

(1985) *Ethics and the Limits of Philosophy* (Cambridge, MA: Harvard University Press).

Wilson, Catherine (1993) 'On Some Alleged Limits to Moral Endeavor'. *The Journal of Philosophy*, 90(6), 275–89.

Wolf, Susan (1982) 'Moral Saints'. *The Journal of Philosophy*, 79(8), 419–39.

Wood, Allen (1999) *Kant's Ethical Thought* (Cambridge: Cambridge University Press).

(2002) 'Preface and Introduction (3–16)'. In Otfried Höffe (ed.), *Immanuel Kant. Kritik der praktischen Vernunft* (Berlin: Akademie Verlag), pp. 25–43.

(2008) *Kantian Ethics* (Cambridge: Cambridge University Press).

(2017) *Formulas of the Moral Law* (Cambridge: Cambridge University Press).

Wood, Allen and Di Giovanni, George (1998) *Kant: Religion within the Boundaries of Mere Reason: And Other Writings (Cambridge Texts in the History of Philosophy)* (Cambridge: Cambridge University Press).

Zhouhuang, Zhengmi (2016) *Der* sensus communis *bei Kant. Zwischen erkenntnis, Moralität, und Schönheit.* (Berlin, Boston, MA: De Gruyter).

Acknowledgements

Over the years I have had many productive discussions about self-deception and rationalizing with a number of outstanding philosophers and/or friends. I wish to thank especially Jens Timmermann, Adrian Piper, Joe Saunders, Anna Wehofsits, James Camien McGuiggan, Kate Moran, Seiriol Morgan, Brian McElwee, Sarah Broadie, Marcia Baron, Stefano Lo Re, Andre Grahle, Laura Papish, Oliver Sensen, Max Jones and Thomas Sturm. I am fully aware that I have subjected some of these individuals to a great deal of rationalizing about my supposed vegetarianism (I used to eat quite a lot of meat for a vegetarian) and other matters. I hope that some of it at least helped them to better understand the depths of human pseudo-rationality. Listening to my own internal laments about the difficulties of being a half-way decent person was certainly an important source of inspiration for this Element.

I am also grateful to Allen Wood for helpful suggestions based on an outline of my project and to Andy Jones for facilitating the review process with exemplary efficiency. Furthermore, I am grateful to the University of Bristol, Brandeis University, the North American Kant Society, the Immanuel Kant Baltic Federal University and the Kantian Rationality Lab based in Kaliningrad for providing me with opportunities to present my material. I am especially grateful to Laura Papish and Jessica Tizzard for a very productive exchange during an ENAKS panel organized by Kate Moran at Brandeis University. Finally, I am grateful to Laura Papish, Anna Wehofsits and Joe Saunders for providing detailed feedback on a draft of my manuscript.

My research was supported by a two-year Irish Research Council Fellowship at Trinity College Dublin (GOIPD/2016/244), a one-term German Academic Exchange Service (DAAD)-funded Guest Chair at the Ruhr-University Bochum and the Ministry of Science and Higher Education of the Russian Federation grant no. 075–15–2019–1929, project 'Kantian Rationality and Its Impact in Contemporary Science, Technology, and Social Institutions', provided at the Immanuel Kant Baltic Federal University (IKBFU), Kaliningrad.

Cambridge Elements ☰

The Philosophy of Immanuel Kant

Desmond Hogan
Princeton University
Desmond Hogan joined the philosophy department at Princeton in 2004. His interests include Kant, Leibniz and German rationalism, early modern philosophy, and questions about causation and freedom. Recent work includes 'Kant on the Foreknowledge of Contingent Truths', Res Philosophica 91 (1) (2014); 'Kant's Theory of Divine and Secondary Causation', in Brandon Look (ed.) *Leibniz and Kant*, Oxford University Press (forthcoming); 'Kant and the Character of Mathematical Inference', in Carl Posy and Ofra Rechter (eds.) *Kant's Philosophy of Mathematics Vol. I*, Cambridge University Press (2020).

Howard Williams
University of Cardiff
Howard Williams was appointed Honorary Distinguished Professor at the Department of Politics and International Relations, University of Cardiff in 2014. He is also Emeritus Professor in Political Theory at the Department of International Politics, Aberystwyth University, a member of the Coleg Cymraeg Cenedlaethol (Welsh-language national college) and a Fellow of the Learned Society of Wales. He is the author of Marx (1980); *Kant's Political Philosophy* (1983); *Concepts of Ideology* (1988); *Hegel, Heraclitus and Marx's Dialectic* (1989); *International Relations in Political Theory* (1992); *International Relations and the Limits of Political Theory* (1996); *Kant's Critique of Hobbes: Sovereignty and Cosmopolitanism* (2003); *Kant and the End of War* (2012) and is currently editor of the journal Kantian Review. He is writing a book on the Kantian legacy in political philosophy for a new series edited by Paul Guyer.

Allen Wood
Indiana University
Allen Wood is Ward W. and Priscilla B. Woods Professor Emeritus at Stanford University. He was a John S. Guggenheim Fellow at the Free University in Berlin, a National Endowment for the Humanities Fellow at the University of Bonn and Isaiah Berlin Visiting Professor at the University of Oxford. He is on the editorial board of eight philosophy journals, five book series and The Stanford Encyclopedia of Philosophy. Along with Paul Guyer, Professor Wood is co-editor of The Cambridge Edition of the Works of Immanuel Kant and translator of the Critique of Pure Reason. He is the author or editor of a number of other works, mainly on Kant, Hegel and Karl Marx. His most recently published books are *Fichte's Ethical Thought*, Oxford University Press (2016) and *Kant and Religion*, Cambridge University Press (2020). Wood is a member of the American Academy of Arts and Sciences.

About the Series
This Cambridge Elements series provides an extensive overview of Kant's philosophy and its impact upon philosophy and philosophers. Distinguished Kant specialists provide an up-to-date summary of the results of current research in their fields and give their own take on what they believe are the most significant debates influencing research, drawing original conclusions.

Cambridge Elements ≡

The Philosophy of Immanuel Kant

Elements in the Series

Formulas of the Moral Law
Allen Wood

Kant's Power of Imagination
Rolf-Peter Horstmann

The Sublime
Melissa McBay Merritt

Kant on Civil Society and Welfare
Sarah Holtman

The Ethical Commonwealth in History: Peace-making as the Moral Vocation of Humanity
Philip J. Rossi

Kant on the Rationality of Morality
Paul Guyer

The Guarantee of Perpetual Peace
Wolfgang Ertl

Kant and Global Distributive Justice
Sylvie Loriaux

Anthropology from a Kantian Point of View
Robert B. Louden

Introducing Kant's Critique of Pure Reason
Paul Guyer and Allen Wood

Kant's Theory of Conscience
Samuel Kahn

Rationalizing (Vernünfteln)
Martin Sticker

A full series listing is available at: www.cambridge.org/EPIK